RELAX
IT'S ONLY
A BABY!

RELAX
IT'S ONLY
A BABY!

DENISE ROBERTSON
ILLUSTRATED BY TREVOR DUNTON

First published in the United Kingdom in 2005 by Little Books Ltd,
48 Catherine Place, London SW1E 6HL

10 9 8 7 6 5 4 3 2 1

A CIP catalogue record for this book is available from the British Library.

ISBN: 1 904435 46 7

The author and publisher will be grateful for any information that will assist them
in keeping future editions up-to-date. Although all reasonable care has been taken in the
preparation of this book, neither the publisher, editors nor the author can accept any liability
for any consequences arising from the use thereof, or the information contained therein.

Many thanks to: Debbie Clement for jacket design and layout conception,
Jamie Ambrose for layout design, editorial production and management,
Claudia Dowell for editing,
Mousemat Design Limited for production consulting and management.
Printed and bound in China.

Contents

INTRODUCTION

Writing this book has made me broody, bringing back those well-remembered sensations of touch and smell, sight and sound of children in the home. If you're reading these words, however, it's likely that you're about to experience all these things for the very first time. If that's the case, you'll probably be excited and apprehensive in equal measure.

For some women, the baby growing within them will be a personality almost from the very moment of conception. They come to know its temperament, its likes and dislikes; they almost know its face. In the nine months these women carry their son or daughter, he or she becomes a friend.

For most of us, though, the child we look down on seconds after it leaves our body is a mysterious stranger, an object of curiosity, awe, affection – and enormous trepidation. A baby changes your life. Nothing will ever be the same again.

Sometimes a child will come into your life through adoption or step-parenthood, or you may be facing parenthood alone. The magic can be the same, but coping must, of necessity, be different. Today's families come in all shapes and sizes, so although this book is designed for parents in any situation, some families may face additional issues.

Whatever your situation may be, there may be times when you will resent the demands your baby makes upon you and your lifestyle. Don't feel guilty about this. The mother who has never looked at her baby and thought *What have I done?* is either a saint or has given birth to one.

Most babies are impatient and, until they get to know and trust you, even dictatorial. But they bring with them a special magic. This book is designed to help you over the bad bits, so that you do not miss a single moment of that magic. In order not to litter these pages with that awkward phrase, 'he or she', I have alternated masculine and feminine pronouns because babies, after all, come in both genders.

Don't expect your child to conform exactly to textbook ideas of what a child should be. Trust your instincts and, above all, take pleasure in your children. Remember, each one of them is unique and therefore special. So are you, their parent.

A child is a gift for life, the only miracle that improves with time. Whatever your circumstances, and whatever type of family you have, make sure you enjoy every step of the way.

PARENTS

The most important resource your baby has is *you*. That is why it is so important that you make time for yourself. It's not selfish; it is the very opposite because you're doing it to protect your baby's future. If your partner has had no experience of babies, he may hesitate to hold his infant, but his hesitation probably has much more to do with fear of such a tiny newcomer than indifference.

Similarly, some partners will enjoy preparing for a coming birth. Others may show less enthusiasm. This is not a sign that they don't care. They may feel ill-equipped to advise or enthuse and so tend to shy away from the subject, but when their baby is in the world they'll feel differently.

Once upon a time men were shut out of labour wards. This was arbitrary and cruel to couples who wanted to share the moment of birth. Now the pendulum has swung to the other extreme and it's almost compulsory for fathers to be there. Discuss this and decide what you both want. If you are to bring up your baby successfully you will need to know when to follow your instincts – and this is a good place to start. If you are both happy with the idea of a joint delivery, that's fine. If not, insist on your right to choose. For

many couples, sharing that moment can
be unbelievably rewarding. For a few, it
is not a joyful experience and they
should resist any pressure to conform.

In the first few days of parenthood
you may wonder quite what you've let yourself in for. Deprived
of sleep, obsessed with 'getting things right', there may be
moments when you feel like running away.

Either one of you may resent the amount of attention given
to the baby, and when you feel like this you feel guilty. Don't
worry; these feelings are temporary and understandable. We're
all human. Once life in the house settles down and the baby is
established in a routine, you'll have time to be man and woman
again – but don't try to establish a routine too soon. Get to
know your baby first.

Try to get as much sleep as you can. This means taking it
when you can get it at first. It can help if you and your partner share night duty; if the off-duty partner can sleep in a separate room, it will make for sounder rest. These emergency
measures won't be needed for more than a few weeks, so don't
worry that the loving companionship of the double bed is
gone forever. The enormous fatigue you may feel in the first
weeks won't last.

Feeding on demand at first allows little or no planning, but soon you'll be moving towards feeding at three-hourly intervals and can get life back on track.

If you're part of a loving relationship, you need to have time together as man and woman, without having one ear cocked for every potential little whimper. If you're on your own, then it's even more important to recharge your batteries. If you push yourself too far, your baby suffers, so nurture yourself as carefully as you nurture your infant.

Build in time for play and laughter, just as you build in those times for your baby. Get plenty of sleep and fresh air and tackle any problems so that you, too, have a healthy, safe environment. Above all, do these things without guilt, because you do them in order to secure your child's future.

Of course, this is all a counsel of perfection. There may not be money for a quiet meal out or a grandma to babysit so you can walk in the countryside. Do what you can, however. If money is tight, try to put aside a little until your treat can be more easily afforded. If babysitting is the main problem, contact Meet a Mum or a similar organization (*see* 'Helpful Organizations & Support Groups', pages 182–7) and try to sort out mutual, occasional child care.

Remember, no one says sex belongs only to bedtime, when you're tired. Occasionally making love in some precious stolen moment can keep your relationship alive. If you can do it when your child is safe elsewhere, all the better.

You're probably both more interested in sleep at this stage, and Mum may still feel a little sore and nervous of resuming sex. Discuss this together and, if necessary, wait until after the six-week check-up. If you want to make love sooner, you can, but remember you will need good contraception. One baby at a time is enough! Don't assume that breast-feeding makes you safe or that the absence of your period makes a difference. Safe sex is your only option.

ADOPTION

Parents who are adopting will have given the matter very careful thought and will be prepared for the advent of a child into their home. The adoption process is lengthy, complicated and often frustrating, but those who make it to the end of the vetting process can be sure they're not acting on impulse. Their children can be sure they were really wanted.

It's very important to be truthful with your child about his origins, and the sooner this becomes an established fact, the better. 'We chose you and you are special' is a good message to impart. Be prepared for questions and, if you can, make it clear that you will not find those questions hurtful. A child will naturally have curiosity about his birth parents but may wonder whether questions will seem disloyal to the adoptive parents he loves.

Remember that the parent who nurtures is the important parent. Your child will learn from your example and return the affection he receives. When conflict arises see it for what it is: the natural friction between child and parent which is part of child development. If you have adopted an older child, don't expect immediate mutual affection; you need to grow together. As you show respect and concern, so the child will relax and feel secure but this process takes time. Most children eligible for adoption have been let down in the past. They will naturally be cautious about giving their trust, but that does not mean that they will never do so. Indeed, the very things that make them cautious, will eventually make them appreciative.

Don't feel that you have to be 'Super-Mum and Dad'. Your new child may have talents and abilities you do not share. As long as you give them the opportunity to achieve their potential, you don't have to drive yourself to play the piano or excel at sport because they do. Glory in your differences – your role is to encourage, not to compete.

It can help to draw a family tree with your child firmly in place. Explain his position in the family and be prepared to talk about that other unknown family. The older child may hint that he needs to know more. There are organizations that will help with these issues and you'll find them in the help section.

A child given in adoption is both a gift and a responsibility. Which makes it exactly like a child born to you in the usual way. If things go wrong or conflict arises never assume it is because that child is not 'yours'. Conflict is natural at times and, in my experience, occurs just as often, if not more often, in the birth situation as it does after adoption.

SINGLE PARENTS

Single parenthood can arise through a broken relationship or the death of a parent. More often than not, the single parent is a mother, but the numbers of single fathers are increasing. Most single parents have to work to support their child and it can be hard to assume the role of sole parent at the end of a working day. Sometimes there is friction with the absent parent or, if there is no other parent living or interested in the child, there are almost constant decisions to take without support or discussion.

The lone parent may be led into the trap of seeing his or her child as another adult, someone with whom to discuss the pros and cons of decisions or share their woes. Although this is understandable, it's not always wise. If you consult frequently it can make it difficult to establish authority when you need to, and it can lead to a child feeling bowed down with responsibility. It increases the bond between parent and child but it also increases dependence of one on the other.

The child may become too concerned over her parent's emotional welfare to voice her own fears or, if money is in short supply, to talk about needs at school or play. And it can create trauma if a new partner appears on the scene. Access to the other parent can assist with this, and grandparents can also play a helpful role. There is also support available from self-help organizations (*see* pages 182–7).

A lone parent should appoint a guardian to care for the child in the event of his or her death. If both parents are alive but separated they can share parental responsibility. This means that each of them has responsibility while the child is in their care but it does not mean they can take life-changing decisions without consulting the other parent.

Although single parenthood can sometimes seem like it's an uphill struggle, the rewards are many. The children of single parents can fare just as well in later life as children from a two-parent family.

Coming Home

Chapter 1

A Word or Two for Mums

Even before you've had your baby, be prepared for a torrent of advice. Almost everyone, it seems, considers themselves a baby expert — including those who have no children of their own. What you must keep in mind is that no one is quite as expert as you are with *this* baby, because she is yours. Be prepared to listen to good advice when it's offered, but always follow your own instincts in the end.

Do try to resist the temptation to buy too much clothing and equipment for your baby before the birth. Your midwife or maternity unit will give you a list of the things you'll really need: it will be minimal. If you're lucky enough to have people who are eager to buy you gifts for your new baby, try and wait to see what has been given. Most gifts in the clothing line will be first-size outfits, and babies grow so quickly it would be a real pity to overbuy.

It's possible that friends may arrange a shower and want to know what you'd like them to give. If so, browse through the baby shops and make a list of things you'd be happy to receive. Include garments in six to twelve months and one-year-up sizes. Weaning and feeding equipment, towels, changing equipment, and toys to aid development are things you might care to add.

Perhaps you gasped with wonder as you saw your baby come into the world. Or maybe you paced the waiting room wondering if life as you knew it was over. Now you find that the house has been taken over by nappies and changing mats. Wind and bowel movements seem to be the sole topic of conversation, and your once-serene partner seems to have more mood swings than the average pendulum.

Well, cheer up, Father. By supporting your partner as much as you can, learning to burp your baby and change his nappy, or rub your other half's weary shoulders, you can help ease the path of adjustment.

Don't be surprised if you have mood swings, too, during this period. At one time you may feel euphoric, at others scared by the responsibility of this new life. This is understandable. What would be very surprising would be if you remained completely unphased by it all. You may feel twinges of resentment towards your change of status. Where has freedom gone? Don't worry; in time the situation will return to normal – with the added bonus of someone who thinks you're the world's best dad.

What You'll Need in the Nursery

- A room thermometer

- A dimmer switch for the light

- A comfortable chair for you to use when feeding

- A cot with a firm mattress

- Changing mat

- A Moses basket or carry-cot

✻ A bowl, cotton wool, barrier cream and nappies

✻ A baby monitor

✻ A car seat

✻ A pushchair – make sure it will fit in your hall or porch

✻ Clothes

BONDING

No doubt you will have heard the word 'bonding' bandied about. It means the instant rapport that is supposed to occur the moment a mother sets eyes on her child. For some mothers that is exactly what happens. With others it takes longer – so don't worry if, for some medical reason, you don't see your child immediately or you don't get that 'instant' feeling.

A baby is pre-programmed to bond and once you have the opportunity to hold her, to feed and get to know her, bonding will come. In fact, it will take awhile before she will be able to differentiate between adults and know who is her mother, so you have time to establish closeness. What is important for emotional well-being and future relationships in adult life is that, in the first few years of life, a child does form a close relationship with at least one adult.

And don't worry that inability to breast-feed will hinder bonding. It's the closeness and the holding of the infant during the feeding process that strengthens the link between mother and baby –nd father and baby, too, for the father who bottle-feeds his baby is also forging valuable links.

It's important to share the early days with your partner or willing grandparents or friends. You will feel a little weary and perhaps overwhelmed. You may feel weepy or extra-sensitive. Don't worry. This is a natural process as your body adjusts to the end of pregnancy. It's known as the baby blues, it usually begins about the third day and it doesn't last.

It's important to remember that what is happening to you is part of the normal emotional spectrum. You are not odd or a failure. Above all, it doesn't mean you don't love your baby or will be a disastrous mother. Try to imagine the hormonal upheaval taking place. Nature prepared you for carrying a baby to full-term. Now, mission accomplished, it is shutting down the system and that takes time. All these feelings are natural. In time your emotions will settle and the blue days dwindle to nothing.

PHOTOGRAPHS

Whether you feel an immediate strong bond with your offspring or not, please don't forget to take photographs of your new arrival. So many changes take place in the first few weeks that you'll be certain to want to look back on them later.

POST-NATAL DEPRESSION

Post-natal depression, a more severe form of the baby-blues, occurs in about fifteen percent of mothers but for many of them it's short-lived. For a few mothers, it can lead to feelings of inadequacy, insomnia, loss of appetite and a disinclination to bond with and care for their baby. The important thing to grasp is that this is a physical condition, probably of hormonal origin, and in no way are you failing as a mother. The condition will respond to treatment with anti-depressants and therapy, and eventually your love affair with your baby will be back on track.

In these early days don't fret about housework. Attend to the essentials, caring for your baby and making sure everyone, including you, eats. And try to have a visitor policy. Everyone will want to see the new baby, but stagger visits and don't feel you have to leap around making tea for everyone.

Lack of sleep is the constant complaint of new parents. Take turns to sleep when you can, whatever the time of day, but remember this stage won't last forever. When you do get

a chance to sleep because someone else is in charge, take yourself right away from the child so that you can't lie with an ear cocked for trouble. This is the moment when Dad can really bond with his son or daughter, giving bottle-feeds of formula or expressed breast milk.

Eventually, you'll develop a routine that will make things easier for you and give your growing child a feeling of security because she knows there are certain landmarks through the day and week. But routine should never be so rigid that it rules your life; certainly in these early days it should not even be considered.

There is no shortage of advice on establishing routine. Books like this one, your midwife, health visitor, your mother or friends who have babies already will be willing and anxious to advise. In the end, though, your routine must be unique, designed by you for your family. You need to recognize that inner voice which says 'Yes, this is the way it should be'.

Listen to advice, weigh it carefully but in the end make your own decision. This is your baby and no one else is quite as well-equipped to care for it.

TWINS

 If you've been gifted with twins you have to adjust feeding, bathing, etc, to accommodate two demands. There are also some special demands on parents due to loss of sleep. Fortunately, there is an organization which can offer good advice where multiple births occur, and details are in the 'Useful Information' section on page 173, but in the meantime, here are some helpful tips.

I believe it's important to treat twins as two children who just happen to have the same birthday. Even identical twins have differing thought processes and personalities, so although it's tempting to see them as two halves of a whole, that can be a mistake.

In the beginning, the prospect of two needy babies can be daunting. It's good to feed them individually whenever you can but if that's not always possible, two big squares of sorbo rubber with a baby-shape scooped out of each one can be positioned either side of you, holding a baby comfortably at each breast. Later, Dad or a trusted adult can feed one while you attend to the other. Don't drive yourself wild with worry over whether or not Baby A

has had ten minutes more of your time
than Baby B, but do try to apportion your
loving equally.

At bath time avoid having both babies in
the water at the same time unless there is another adult on
hand. In the second it takes to lift one child out and carry it
to another room, its sibling could drown. If you're on your
own bring a high chair into the bathroom and let one baby
watch from safety while the other is in the water. Baby shops
are geared to deal with multiple birth requirements and you'll
soon adjust to the practical demands of twins.

There is no doubt that there is a bond between children who
have shared a womb, but they should be encouraged to explore
their differing potential and have separate circles of friends.
Too often, parents assume twins will be enough for each other
and make less effort to encourage friendships outside the home.
Later, in their school lives, twins may need to go separate ways;
if they are used to socializing independently, this
will be easier.

It may be necessary to have a shared wardrobe
in the early days but, where possible, let them
develop individual tastes in dress. Spend time

alone with each child when you can and make sure that both get to make choices. Try not to refer to them as 'the twins'. Loving parents referring to their family of four children will say 'Peter and John and the twins' when they should say 'Peter and John and Mary and Margaret.'

Often one twin will be more vocal and outgoing than the other and will almost dictate events for both of them. This is a natural process and not a fault in the dominant one, but if parents aren't careful, the less outgoing twin can become almost a shadow of her stronger sibling.

The pleasure of seeing two children with a shared bond more than makes up for the extra work, so don't let the prospect of multiple birth depress you.

CRYING

CHAPTER 2

THE CRYING GAME

It is natural for your newborn to cry. It is his only means of communication. Research suggests that babies cry for about two hours a day during the first few weeks and then taper off as parents anticipate their needs.

When crying starts, check to see if your baby's nappy needs changing or whether he needs feeding. Is he too hot or cold or in an uncomfortable position? A baby who has wind and tummy pain will draw up his knees and the cry will be more piercing.

Talk in a reassuring way or pick the baby up for a cuddle. Walking with him in your arms or pushing him in a pram helps. Don't make the mistake of thinking he is crying because you have let him down in some way. Crying is natural so keep your cool. Eventually the crying will cease, the baby will sleep and you can have a nice cup of tea.

If you feel at the end of your tether, make the baby comfortable, then go into another room for a while. If the crying has persisted for too long, try calming him with a gentle massage. If you feel you can't cope, contact one of the helplines listed on pages 182–7. They will understand.

No baby cries for fun or to give you a hard time. At this early stage crying is the only way he has to communicate. He is sending you a message in a language you have yet to learn. In time you'll understand and know just what to do to right the situation. When you respond, speak calmly and lovingly. It doesn't matter what you say as long as your tone is soothing. That affectionate voice says, 'Message received and understood,' allowing your baby to relax.

What's Making Her Cry?

 Hungry

 Needs a nappy change

 Wind

 Tired

 Too cold

Too hot

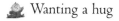 Wanting a hug

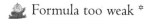 Formula too weak *

Breast milk unsatisfactory *

 Unwell *

    * Your health visitor or doctor will help here.

FEEDING

CHAPTER 3

BREAST- OR BOTTLE-FEEDING?

It's universally acknowledged that 'breast is best', as breast-milk provides perfect nutrition and some immunity against infection. However, some mothers are not able to breast-feed, while others choose not to do so. It's important to make this decision for yourself and not be persuaded to breast-feed or bottle-feed against your will.

Talk to your midwife and, if you possibly can, give breast-feeding a try. Babies benefit even from a couple of weeks of breast-feeding; you can switch to a bottle later if you choose.

Both methods, properly applied, are good for your baby. In my opinion, the idea that breast-feeding makes for a closer bond is untrue. It's the holding and satisfying that forges the link between parent and child.

BREAST-FEEDING WILL:

Provide everything needed for health and development; be easy to digest and cause fewer tummy upsets or constipation; protect your baby from infections and perhaps from developing eczema later; help a mother regain her figure as it uses up fat stored during pregnancy. It's also cheap, available twenty-four hours a day and gives premature babies the very best start. Others can feed your baby using expressed breast milk.

BOTTLE-FEEDING WILL:

Allow Dad to share the feeding and make it easier to leave your baby with his dad, grandparents or other trusted relatives and friends. Bottle-feeding also takes less time to feed but more time to prepare — and, unfortunately, it costs money. This method of feeding also offers less protection for your baby against tummy upsets, allergies and infections.

THE ART OF BREAST-FEEDING

Don't assume that breast-feeding is a simple matter of placing baby to nipple. At the beginning it can be hard work, as both you and baby get the hang of it, and may take three weeks or more to be established. For the first day or two, your breasts provide a thick yellow liquid called colostrum, which is especially valuable. Your midwife will help you, so don't be afraid to ask questions.

Initially, your breasts may be uncomfortable, and as your baby realizes what a good thing he's onto he may suck so vigorously that he gets a 'sucking blister' on his lip. Don't worry; these conditions soon disappear and feeding becomes a source of pleasure for both mother and baby.

If you develop sore nipples, ask your midwife or doctor for help. Positioning the baby correctly eases pressure on the nipple and you'll quickly learn to get the position right. Expressing a little milk before each feed can help and also helps to avoid painful mastitis — inflamed or blocked milk ducts. A hot shower or bath prior to feeding can help the flow of milk. Alternatively, a packet of frozen peas placed on the breast can ease discomfort. Try not to stop breast-feeding and turn to using a bottle as this won't help your milk flow. Breast-feeding works by supply and demand. The more your baby takes, the more you'll produce.

Feed your baby frequently at first, changing breasts at the next feed. And don't worry if he stops for a little rest now and then. It's a good opportunity to help him burp by holding him upright against your shoulder and gently rubbing or patting his back.

Alternatively, you can express milk and feed baby later. Ask your midwife to show you how to do this and store the milk safely in the refrigerator.

There will be plenty of time to get into a routine once feeding is established. If your breasts leak, try using breast-pads in your bra and be sure to change them often.

Regular weighing will tell you if all is well with your child, but remember that babies usually lose weight in the first few days and make it up later. Remember to look after yourself, too, and make sure you get lots of support and encouragement during these early, complicated weeks.

TIPS FOR HAPPY FEEDING

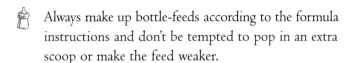 Always make up bottle-feeds according to the formula instructions and don't be tempted to pop in an extra scoop or make the feed weaker.

Always wash your hands before feeding and wash bottles and teats thoroughly, using a bottle brush. Old milk harbours germs. Special bottle-cleaning kits can be purchased at the chemist.

Give cooled, boiled water between feeds if your baby is thirsty and make sure the teat is the right size. Teats that are too big or too small can cause wind.

 When bottle-feeding, always keep the teat full of milk so that baby doesn't suck in air, and wind carefully several times during each feed, just as you do when breast-feeding. Do this thoroughly as wind can cause tummy pain and disturbed sleep.

 At first, you should feed on demand, but as the weeks go by this settles into three feeds a day and later on you can use breast and bottle if you choose. When he's thirsty, offer cooled, boiled water or natural fruit juice, well-diluted.

 And enjoy feeding times, whether bottle or breast, as moments of tranquillity before weaning begins.

NAPPIES

CHAPTER 4

THE BOTTOM LINE

Make life easier for yourself by keeping all you need for nappy changing in a bag which goes wherever the baby goes. That means you don't have to run up and down stairs looking for baby wipes or disposal bags. The easier you make things, the more time you'll have to enjoy watching your baby.

Always keep a wad of cotton wool handy if you're changing a baby boy. In the early days, a baby boy is apt to pee as soon as his penis is uncovered and his aim is far-reaching! Always wipe your baby girl front to back to prevent bacteria from her anus getting near her vagina. And don't worry about the colour of early motions: if you're breast-feeding, what you've eaten can influence the shade. If constipation is the problem, give very diluted orange juice and extra water. Always consult your doctor or health visitor if you're really worried about the contents of a nappy, but remember: there is no absolute norm.

When you've removed the soiled nappy, clean your infant's bottom thoroughly with baby wipes or soap and water, paying particular attention to the creases. Dry thoroughly and apply barrier cream before putting on the new nappy.

If you want to use terry nappies, you'll need at least two dozen. Disposable nappies may seem more expensive, but you won't need plastic pants, nappy liners and laundry equipment, so the difference in cost isn't huge – although the cost to the environment in terms of landfill use may well be a factor in your final decision. Terry nappies need soaking in a bucket of diluted sterilizing fluid after the contents have been disposed of. Disposable nappies come with a bag to put them in ready for disposal.

Always wash your hands after changing nappies, especially after your baby has had a polio jab, as the live virus will be in the baby's stools for about a month.

A GUIDE TO NAPPY CHANGING

Keep everything you need together.

Keep cotton wool handy.

Make sure you have a safe, steady surface for baby to lie on.

Remove soiled nappy and bag for disposal.

Thoroughly cleanse baby's bottom with wipes or soap and water.

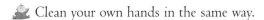 Clean your own hands in the same way.

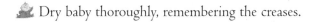 Dry baby thoroughly, remembering the creases.

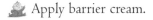 Apply barrier cream.

Put on new nappy.

Adjust baby's clothing and give her a cuddle.

Wash your hands again thoroughly.

SLEEPING

CHAPTER 5

THE SNOOZE NEWS

New babies sleep for about sixteen hours a day. Unfortunately, they don't have a sense of night and day so you need to catch your sleep whenever you can. Of course, it's a temptation to hold your baby all the time, but instead rock her in her crib or push the pram back or forth until she nods off. Remember always to put her on her back.

Gradually, you can move her naps to the times of the day that suit your routine. Don't make bedtime too early at first and, with luck, you may get a few hours of sleep at normal times. As your baby develops, sleep patterns change; we will deal with this later.

WHY BABIES DON'T SLEEP

The reasons why a tiny baby won't sleep are easily dealt with. She may be hungry or her nappy may need changing. Very possibly it's wind, which needs gentle encouragement to emerge as a burp. Sometimes a bedroom that is too warm or too cold can be the trouble, or there may be too much light in the room. She may just need a cuddle.

If there are no symptoms of an ailment, sickness, diarrhoea or listlessness, and baby isn't hot or sweating, try leaving her to cry for a few moments. Chances are she'll relax and fall asleep. If not, you can always go back and comfort her. If this is happening regularly, make sure you're not putting her to bed when she's wide awake or has had too much sleep during the day.

SLEEP WHEN YOU CAN

In those first few months, sleep whenever she sleeps; it may only be for an hour or two but it helps. And don't feel guilty about going to bed at noon – be grateful for the chance! However bad things get, don't be tempted to let her share your bed; she could wriggle under the covers and overheat. And it's a difficult habit to break.

After three months a pattern should emerge. You'll know when to put her down and you'll probably only have to feed once during the night. This is when you can think about moving her cot into her own room; however, most mums prefer to wait until six months, when sleep problems will be over.

WHY WON'T HE SLEEP?

- Is he hungry?

- Does he need changing?

- Could he be teething?

- Is the room temperature right?

- Is he correctly dressed?

- Does he have a sore bottom?

CREATE THE RIGHT ATMOSPHERE

Before bedtime it pays to quieten things down. If Dad wants to play with his son or daughter when he gets home, time bedtime for half an hour after the high jinks. In that half-hour make sure you give plenty of cuddles but not too much stimulation. When you put him down gently, pat him. He may cry at first so sing quietly but don't pick him up.

If he wakes in the night offer a gentle cuddle as you settle him down, but no fun and games. He needs to get the message that nightime is for sleeping. Feed and change him and then put him down again.

ESTABLISH A ROUTINE

At around six months, your ideal routine is tea, quiet time, bath and bed, but make it all a pleasant, unrushed affair. Of course he may resist. Your baby is developing a mind of his own and knows what he wants. Don't be discouraged. Be loving and gentle, soothe him if necessary but stick to the routine. This may mean there will be times when you must sit by his cot for quite a while when you're longing to go back to the living-room and relax. Believe me, it will be worth it. Good habits formed now will last.

SETTLING DOWN

As the days go by, you'll need to spend less and less time at your baby's side, but don't simply leave him alone abruptly. Position your chair away from the cot for a day or two, then by the door. And don't worry about faint noise from the living room, unless it's obvious that this is causing problems. Some babies actually find this type of background noise soothing; it's normally only sharp and unexpected noises that disturb them.

Gradually, your baby's daytime naps will become shorter as he sleeps longer at night. It's wise to try to have him take them before 3.30 in the afternoon.

WHEN PROBLEMS ARISE

If, after good sleep patterns have been well and truly established, there's a setback, don't panic. Go to your baby if he cries, but don't make a fuss. Go through your checklist on page 56 and, if all is well, settle him down, pat him gently and leave him. Pop in and out of his bedroom, but don't pick him up. It's hard to hear him cry, but as long as you're sure there's nothing really wrong, stick it out. And remember: you're not alone. Your health visitor is there to consult if you're desperate.

If you decide painful teething is the problem because your little one has swollen red gums, flushed cheeks and perhaps a temperature, give him baby paracetamol or a similar product recommended by your health visitor or GP, or rub his gums with a teething gel.

A sore bottom can be soothed with cream.

Sometimes your baby's growing curiosity will lead to restlessness. Even a tired baby can be curious about what he's missing. You can see him struggle to stay awake and, as he grows, try to command attention. Accept this as a welcome sign of development but don't be swayed by it. Your baby needs sleep and you need time off.

Above all, don't give up and return him to the family circle. Do this once and your baby will aim for it every time.

BATHING

CHAPTER 6

Good Clean Fun

For first-time parents, bath time can be both a delight and an ordeal. Holding a wet, slippery and perhaps screaming infant can be terrifying. Don't worry. You don't have to immerse the baby every time. Have a medium-size plastic bowl and use your elbow to test the water.

Choose a time when your baby is happy and not newly fed and then keep her in a towel on your knee. Wash, face, neck and hands, using a damp cotton wool ball to wipe around eyes from the nose outward. Use a separate ball for each eye and one for each ear but don't clean inside the ear or let water enter there. Wash face and neck, getting into all the creases and drying as you go.

Wash her hands and use a wet cotton-wool ball to clean the navel area. The cord will shrivel and drop off after about a week. Dry each area as you go. Last of all remove her nappy and wash her bottom, getting into all the creases and drying well. (If your baby is a boy, it's not necessary to pull back the foreskin.) You can then lower her gently into the bath and allow her to kick.

If there are signs of nappy rash use barrier cream on the whole area. If nappy rash persists, make sure you are changing your baby often enough and mention the problem to your health visitor or GP.

As your confidence increases you can use baby bath liquid and shampoo. Wash face and hands as before, then wrap the baby in a towel and hold her in the crook of your left arm with her head over the bath. You can then gently wash and rinse her hair without water reaching her eyes. Don't worry about the fontanelles – the two soft spots on the baby's head. The back fontanelle closes up at about six weeks. The front one doesn't close until about eighteen months but the skin over them is tough and you needn't fear damaging them.

Next, soap baby all over except the face. If you've used baby bath liquid, soap is unnecessary. Lower her gently into the bath, your right arm under her and holding her right arm, and allow her to kick about in the water. Use your free hand to scoop the water over her till all the soap is removed. As the weeks pass, both baby and you will enjoy this more and more.

When it's time to leave the bath, lift her onto the towel on your knee and dry thoroughly, paying special attention to the creases. A gentle massage with baby oil is the perfect finish.

BATHING A NEW BABY

- Assemble everything you need and make sure you have a comfortable chair at the right height.

- Use a medium-sized bowl.

- Always test the water with your elbow.

- Undress your baby and wrap her in a towel on your knee.

- Wash face, neck and hands, using damp cotton-wool balls.

- Wipe her eyes from nose outward, using a separate ball for each eye.

- Dry thoroughly, remembering the creases.

 Use a wet cotton ball to clean the navel area.

Remove nappy and clean her bottom as usual.

Lower baby gently into water, your right arm under her, your right hand holding her right arm.

Allow her to kick, gently scooping water over her with your left hand.

Lift out and dry her thoroughly.

Apply barrier cream as usual.

A gentle massage with baby oil is the perfect finish if you have time.

GROWING

CHAPTER 7

DEVELOPMENT

Because every child is unique, all children will reach the different stages of development at their own pace. However, this is a rough guide to the progress your baby will make as he or she grows towards school age.

AT BIRTH

Your baby is aware of changes in temperature, bright lights, being handled and the comfort and closeness of another human body. He has no control over his own body because his nervous system is not yet sufficiently developed. His head is disproportionate to his body, his legs are small and weak and all he can do for himself is breathe, suck, turn his head a little and cry. Can you blame him that he exercises his lungs vigorously from time to time?

A new baby may put his fingers to his mouth and likes being upright because he can see more clearly than when he is lying down. He is startled by sudden noises and doesn't like the sensation of falling, so always lower him gently into cot or pram. But very soon after the birth he recognizes the nipple or the teat and will show excitement when put to the breast. He sleeps about sixteen to eighteen hours and feeds about ten times a day.

ONE MONTH

Your baby has settled into a routine. She has discovered that she can exercise her hands and enjoys spreading her fingers, sucking a thumb or even a fist. Her arms will stretch out occasionally and sometimes the fingers of one hand will explore the other. Similarly, when free from nappy and clothing the legs will move, toes will spread and wiggle and your baby may begin to lift her head for a second, especially when held against your shoulder. Her eyes will follow objects moving close to her face and she will be soothed by the human voice – except when she's hungry and refuses to be pacified.

Above all, the month-old baby will appreciate security, warmth and the sensation of being loved. She can meet your gaze and smile and knows her mother by smell and sound.

A personality is emerging now. Your baby is alert and enjoys company. He will smile and make noises other than crying and will try to roll onto his side. He kicks with his legs and enjoys pushing with his feet against the foot of the pram or cot or his mother's hands. He enjoys being walked in Mother or Father's arms and wants to be part of the company but will lie contentedly in his cot after feeding, kicking and gurgling. Remember, all babies are different.

If your baby hates to lie down or to be left for a second, don't despair. All phases pass with time. And if your baby was smaller than usual at birth, don't worry. There will be a gradual catching-up process and by school age there will be little or no difference.

SIX MONTHS

Your baby will have doubled her birth weight and grown about five inches. She can wriggle about on her stomach or sit up in her pram, propped against a cushion. She can handle toys now and loves to wave them about. She practises sounds and will enjoy your oohs and aahs of approval. She will try to support herself on her legs and pull herself up on furniture, she chews everything she can find because her teeth are almost ready to emerge. She likes to have toys offered to her and will offer them back but is not yet able to open her grasp and let go.

She loves to be bounced on someone's knee and enjoys being sung to or engaged in conversation. At this stage, she can now recognize 'her' people: family, siblings or friends. However, she will not immediately smile at strangers, only responding when she is sure they are friendly.

Nine months

This is the time to move your ornaments to a higher shelf. Your baby is mobile now, can crawl from place to place and will be attracted to things like trailing flex or objects he can handle and put in his mouth. Make sure the home is child-safe so that you can relax and watch your baby explore. It may take time to child-proof every room but it's easier in the end than frustrating your baby by jumping up every few minutes to take something away from him.

He will enjoy family times, especially the more boisterous ones, kicking and moving his body to show delight. Bath times are especially pleasurable, and simple scoops and cartons will give endless enjoyment.

By now he will probably be having three meals a day. He can hold his own mug with two hands and will try to grab and wield the spoon. If his mother doesn't allow him the use of the spoon it may produce a temper tantrum and a stiffening of his whole body. The answer is to provide a second spoon. You make sure a sufficient amount of food gets eaten. He 'feeds' himself and doesn't at all mind that most of it ends up on his bib.

TWELVE MONTHS

At one year old your baby can pull himself up on the furniture and then move sideways. He can let go and stand for a minute or may even stagger forward if you hold his hand. He can use his thumb and forefinger as pincers and can now let go of things at will. This means he can throw things out of the pram or cot and this usually becomes a favourite game. He chatters away, using words like 'ma-ma' or 'dad-dad', and will now play alone quite happily although he likes to know Mum or Dad are near.

He is more accepting of strangers, especially if they are willing to play peek-a-boo, and understands simple words like 'bath' and 'walk', even if he can not repeat them.

Your child will concentrate on improving her mobility, negotiating stairs, walking, balancing, climbing chairs and moving her toys, especially if they have wheels. Once she has mastered movement she will concentrate on speech. She wants the undivided attention of her mother or carer and will resort to crying if ignored. Independence assumes enormous importance now. She wants to feed herself and will only allow herself to be dressed if the process is quick. There is so much to do and explore that fastening buttons and straps seems a waste of time.

She is fascinated by fitting things together and putting one object inside another. Toys get rough treatment now, especially if they don't do what is wanted. Although control of bowels and bladder is still far off, it helps to introduce a potty which can be used on the odd occasion that Mum sees a poo or wee coming in time.

Words come easily now, and by the time of the second birthday your daughter's vocabulary will encompass up to two hundred words.

Up to three years

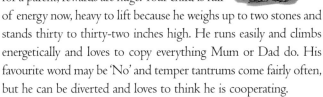

Although the third year is physically demanding for a parent, rewards are huge. Your child is full of energy now, heavy to lift because he weighs up to two stones and stands thirty to thirty-two inches high. He runs easily and climbs energetically and loves to copy everything Mum or Dad do. His favourite word may be 'No' and temper tantrums come fairly often, but he can be diverted and loves to think he is cooperating.

This is a time when nightmares may occur or fear of the dark begins. Don't be alarmed by these fears. They are symptoms of his developing imagination, and with comfort and reassurance they will pass. Be tolerant, too, of what may appear to be temper tantrums. He has learned to be angry but not yet how to control his anger. He is worried by unusual occurrences, like Mum not being where he expected her to be and he is horrified by what seems like anger or distress in a loved one. And he does not yet know that what occurs in dreams is imaginary.

The third year isn't all gloom. The comedian in your child begins to emerge. He enjoys dressing up, making you laugh, playing word or finger games and, as his third birthday approaches, 'helping' in family rituals like tidying up or table laying. He will probably have daytime control of bladder and bowels and be proud of using his potty. By two-and-a-half or so, he will have a full set of milk teeth.

BEYOND TODDLERHOOD

By the time your child reaches four years of age, most babyhood problems will have gone. There may still be some night-time bedwetting or the occasional daytime accident, but these are best treated lightly.

Your daughter will run and jump, ride a tricycle and climb with confidence. She can use pencil and crayons and cut with child-proof scissors, but more precise finger movements will still be difficult. Her favourite words will be 'what', 'where' and 'how' and there will be a new word everyday.

The companionship of other children becomes all-important now, and the essential lessons of sharing and taking turns come into play. In the absence of other children, toys become 'people'. Dolls are bathed and dressed or treated for 'poorly tummies' and rows of toy figures become armies to be advanced upon. At nursery or playgroup, the three-year-old also learns that adults outside the family can be trusted.

The four-year-old child is keen on independence, but will respond to reason. Holding hands to cross a busy road or in crowds makes sense as long as he is not so constrained when safety is reached. He knows when adults behave unfairly and he likes an apology. He can control his emotions and will show a great deal of patience when making a construction out of his toy building bricks.

He may have a 'special friend' now, but will turn to a parent or teacher for help when needed. Your son can now find things out for himself. Even small children can use picture encyclopedias or computers, but if the answer cannot be found there, an adult who will help is essential.

Sometimes the personality of a four-year-old may seem to change. They may become bossy or aggressive, enjoy disobeying or being rude or silly. This can simply be independence taken too far or it may be boredom. Be tolerant, use diversions and concentrate on showing your child respect.

Giving the rebel a task to carry out, such as feeding the rabbit, will produce a better result than a lecture or a threat of retribution.

Watch out, too, for signs of apprehension of school. Some children look forward to school as a huge adventure. For others the prospect is too daunting and they need reassurance.

TALKING

CHAPTER 8

CONVERSATION

I was once reprimanded by an aunt for using 'baby talk' to my infant son, 'He won't be able to speak properly when he grows up,' she said. She was wrong. Before long I was wondering how to stop an extremely articulate toddler from talking non-stop.

Talk to your child from the moment of birth in the way that seems natural to you. Some mothers croon a language of their own. Others recite nursery rhymes. The words don't matter. The baby knows it is being addressed and that is the important issue.

Your voice should bring an almost immediate response from your baby; failure to react by turning towards you or gurgling in return could indicate a hearing loss. If this happens, don't panic — even small babies may day-dream — but if it happens repeatedly or loud noises fail to startle her, mention it to your health visitor. Use your voice to soothe your baby when she is fretful and, as the baby develops, show pleasure at the sounds she makes for you.

At around two months your baby will show a desire to communicate verbally. Encourage this. You'll be amazed at how much they convey by gurgling.

Some experts believe children have an innate ability to learn a language and there's no doubt that children who grow up in a verbally rich environment learn faster. Your baby will start to imitate your sounds. A particular favourite may be 'B' or 'M'. Have fun with sounds.

You'll probably find you are using 'Motherese', a way of speaking slowly and distinctly with spaces between the words: 'Where...is...my...lovely...baby...girl?' Motherese has a rhythm to it, which a baby likes, and it contains a lot of repetition, which is comforting.

Most experts like my reprimanding aunt disapprove of using 'baby language', words like 'moo-moo' and 'bow-wow'. It's better to use proper words such as 'cow' and 'dog', but if 'bow-wow' and 'gee-gee' come naturally to your lips don't be afraid of them or worry that you're doing harm. What is important is that you and your baby should enjoy conversing. Don't forget to listen attentively even when the sounds don't make sense. Without that encouragement why should your baby bother to learn to speak?

As your baby becomes a toddler, talk through everyday routines. 'Here is your lunch.' 'Good, you seem to like that.' 'Shall we put on your new dress?' Simple phrases like these, especially when you hold up the object, are helping your child begin the ascent of language; a mountain of words, some with more than one meaning. The sooner you start chatting to her, the better. And don't forget action rhymes like 'Round and Round the Garden'. The look of pleasure on the face of the smallest child as she waits for the familiar punchline of a gentle tickle is a glorious sight.

Enjoy picture books together, pointing out objects and naming them or, better still, waiting for your child to name them. To a child, reading the same story again and again is reassuring, so stifle your yawns and content yourself with introducing new books from time to time.

It's important to encourage your child to listen. Even at an early stage you can help him develop the ability to obey requests and absorb information, abilities which will be invaluable later on in nursery and school.

Don't scatter commands that don't need to be obeyed; they only confuse. But when you say 'Please come here,' make sure your child does come, putting out a welcoming hand if necessary. Remember that even a very young child likes to understand the reason for such requests. Saying 'Please come here because…' will produce a better reaction than 'Do it because I say so.'

At about three, a child's language increases in both volume and complexity. We've all heard the harassed mother in the supermarket begging her child not to ask one more blankety-blank question! Understanding how your child sees the world around him will help you find the necessary patience to answer those questions in a straightforward way. Don't be afraid to say 'I don't know,' but recognize that is only a temporary answer. Say instead, 'I don't know, but when we get home we'll find out.' Psychologists believe the use of a child's name helps it absorb new information, so when you ask Daddy or Gran if they know the answer, personalize the question if you can. For example, 'Paula wants to know why her ball is round,' is more relevant to your child than 'Why is a ball round?'

Sometimes questions can be difficult, especially when they concern vital matters such as sex and death. I think truth is important, but that doesn't mean you have to explain the fine details of the *Kama Sutra* to the three-year-old who simply asks, 'Where do babies come from?'

Above all, remember that language, as with everything else, develops at different rates in different children. Some children will string words together fluently at eighteen months. Others may reach that stage at three. Girls tend to develop language skills sooner than boys, but early talkers are not necessarily more intelligent than late talkers. However, if your child isn't forming some words by age two, it may indicate hearing difficulties and should be investigated.

Going Out

Chapter 9

PUBLIC DEBUT

The prospect of taking your baby out into the world can be daunting but a baby should enhance your life, not constrict it. Occasionally, you will be able to leave him with Gran or a trusted friend but there will be other times when you need to go out on your own and want to take him with you.

When you are ready to venture out, lay your baby flat in his pram – it's too soon to prop him up. If you're taking him out in the car you need a properly secured, backward-facing baby seat or carry cot with safety straps. For trips to the shops, a baby sling is ideal until he gets too heavy for comfort.

In cold weather your baby need a hat, but take outer clothes off when you take him inside (even inside the car) and put them on again for going out. In summer be sure to protect him from the sun. Use a sun block cream and a lightweight sun hat. Never leave the baby lying in the sun and use a canopy on the pram.

One worry is infection. The world can seem full of coughs and sneezes and you are anxious to shield your baby from every possible germ. In fact, keeping a baby in a sterile environment isn't beneficial. Sooner or later he will have to join the world and introducing him slowly and sensibly is the way to do it.

There's another reason why contact with the outside world is vital. I have never forgotten walking up to the pram of a close friend, wanting to admire her baby. My approach was gentle but the poor baby screamed in terror at the sight of me. 'She's not used to seeing people,' her mother said apologetically. Imagine the trauma for that baby if Mum had been hospitalized or called away suddenly and strangers had appeared to take over the baby's care. Your baby needs to know the world is a friendly place, so when you are ready to take a trip don't hesitate.

Of course I'm not suggesting you throw your baby and spare nappies into the back of the car and take off for Uzbekistan. You need to know all about the place you're going to and you need to take everything your baby will need with you. Plan thoroughly, make lists and above all make sure that whatever your baby travels in is designed for the job. An unsecured carry-cot on the back seat of a car is not a good idea!

One word of warning. Never, ever leave your baby in the car, not even for a second. And that's a rule for home as well as away.

HOLIDAYS

Most holiday resorts at home and abroad are used to catering for babies, and travel agents should be able to tell you exactly what facilities you can expect. With a very young child it's unwise to roam too far from the beaten track and easy access to hospitals, etc, although there's no reason why your baby should be more at risk away from home if you've planned sensibly.

There may be minor problems with settling down in a strange environment but these usually disappear after the first or second night. Of course, water should always be boiled and you need to be extra-careful when preparing your baby's food but don't be paranoid about it.

PARTIES

It can be frustrating to sit at home when your friends are partying and you can't find a babysitter. Taking a baby into a loud and possibly smoky atmosphere is not a good idea, but a small baby can be settled in a Moses basket or carry-cot in a friend's bedroom and, once asleep, slumber soundly through the party and the ride home.

It's more difficult once your baby becomes a toddler so cultivate reliable babysitters but don't feel your social life is gone beyond recall. It's usually possible to join in for at least part of the evening and most people are very willing to accommodate your needs, especially if they have children themselves.

EATING OUT

A lot of restaurants have special arrangements for families in the early part of the evening. Babies love the atmosphere, especially now that restaurants have no-smoking policies. Take along something for your baby to nibble and don't be scared to ask for hot water to heat a bottle.

When I used to travel alone with a young baby, eating out was difficult, unless it was sleeping time. Trying to eat your meal with your baby on your knee is almost impossible once the sitting-up stage is reached. But, however much you long for assistance, handing your baby over to strangers, however helpful, is scary. Of course, you should never let your baby out of your sight, but if someone offers to sit at your table and amuse the baby while you eat, don't turn them down flat. After all, wouldn't you wish to be helpful if the position were reversed? Like so many others things, it's a matter of judgement. Don't be afraid to accept help. Equally, don't be afraid to say a polite 'No, thank you' if you feel uneasy.

WEANING

CHAPTER 10

IS HE READY FOR SOLIDS?

He could be, if he looks wistfully at what you're eating; breast or bottle doesn't seem to satisfy; he's four months old (if your baby was born prematurely then this stage will come a little later).

Once you decide your baby is ready to be weaned, assemble the things you'll need for solids. You will need:

- Plastic bibs
- A high chair

- Bowls and spoons
- A sterilizer

- A trainer cup
- Lots of patience

- A blender

The introduction of new foods is a gradual process and as breast- and bottle-fed babies are already getting a balanced diet, there is no need to worry if your baby rejects these new tastes at first; he will not go undernourished.

The night feeds should begin to diminish once he is six months old, and they will be the hardest for your baby to give up. Make that feed gradually shorter and put a milky drink in his feeder cup. That and plenty of cuddles should do the trick. If you're going from breast to feeder cup, it's best to get someone else to introduce it so that your baby doesn't smell your breast milk and feel frustrated. This is when Dad can be useful, sorting his offspring if he wakes. If you go to your baby, he'll smell your milk and get his hopes up. Don't put a firm limit on night feeds. Together you can gradually work towards a good night's sleep for all the family.

In the early stages avoid commercial puréed baby foods as your baby needs to get ready for ordinary food. Eventually your infant will be having three meals a day, and snacks such as fresh fruit, rice cakes or raw carrot in between. Cottage cheese, yoghurt, and unsweetened fromage frais can be used or a little grated cheese added to other foods. Avoid sweet biscuits, chocolates and cakes and don't add sugar to cereals. It's best not to give cow's milk as the main milk drink during the weaning stage; your baby is still having formula or breast milk. Where you do mix cow's milk with cereals, it should be full-fat.

Don't worry if your baby doesn't move from stage to stage in the 'normal' time frame. As we have already noted, every baby is different.

Mealtimes should be fun for you both. Remember that your baby's brain is growing, too. He'll quickly learn that he can worry you by refusing food or throwing it around so don't rise to the bait. A poker face is your best weapon.

When you stop breast-feeding is up to you, but it gets more difficult to stop as your son gets older and can assert his will. As long as you and your baby are happy with the decision, it's fine to stop at any time short of nursery or school time. But do it well before another baby comes along as this could make number one feel jealous and deprived.

When you're ready to stop breast or bottle, it's time for the feeder cup. Introduce it gradually, at times when he's thirsty and will be keen to drink.

HOMEMADE IS BEST

You can purée fruit and vegetables and freeze in ice-cube trays. One cube of food a day unfrozen and warmed is enough at first. Commercial foods such as baby rice or broth are fine if you're in a hurry, but choose those which are gluten-free and without added sugar. Remember that cooled, boiled water is an essential part of your baby's diet.

Initially, don't give wheat-based foods such as pasta and avoid lumpy food. And remember not to use salt or sugar or anything fried. Avoid anything too sweet as this can lead to a dislike of anything that isn't sweet.

Don't worry if your baby rejects a particular food or, as he gets older, decides he'd rather paint it on everything, including you. Allow him to use a spoon when he's ready. Of course he'll make a mess but this is an important part of his development.

Next will come finger foods. He'll enjoy having a piece of melon or apple or a crust of bread even before he has teeth to chew with. But never leave him alone with anything he could choke on. At about six months he'll enjoy feeding in his high chair. Mealtimes can be really pleasant then as you sit eye to eye and make conversation but dress accordingly – it can be a messy business.

By now he'll enjoy minced or mashed family foods such as meat, fish, chicken or beans, but again no salt or spices. Well-cooked omelettes will go down well, too, and there's no need to avoid food containing gluten.

Children over one year old should be given whole milk in preference to skimmed or semi-skimmed (these can be given after the fifth birthday).

WHAT DOES A CHILD NEED?

Proportionally, children need more protein than adults because their basic body tissue is growing quickly. Animal protein comes from eggs and dairy produce, meat and fish. Vegetable protein is derived from cereals, nuts, root vegetables and pulses. Carbohydrates, which produce energy, are present in sugary foods and starchy foods like bread and potatoes. Some carbohydrate is essential, but eaten to excess it turns into body fat. The same is true of fat, which is found in meat, fish oil, butter and margarine and some vegetables.

Fibre, sometimes called roughage, encourages digestion and discourages constipation. It is found in fruit and vegetables, wholemeal bread, wholegrain cereals, nuts and pulses. Check the content of breakfast cereals carefully to make sure that the beneficial effects of the fibre they contain are not outweighed by the salt and sugar content.

Vitamins and minerals are essential and can only be derived from food. Children need vitamin A, found in cheese, fish, eggs, chicken, spinach and carrots. Vitamin B comes from milk, liver, cheese and wholemeal bread, while vitamin C is found in fresh fruit and vegetables, especially citrus fruits. Vitamin D is found in fish oil, liver, dairy produce and sunshine, and vitamin E can be derived from oats, brown rice, liver, wholegrain cereals and nuts.

Minerals such as calcium are found in milk, cheese, yoghurt and green vegetables. Iron comes from red meat, eggs, bread and green vegetables. Don't be alarmed by such a long list of requirements. A child's needs are small and many foods provide most or several things at once.

WEANING IN STAGES

Weaning is necessary to provide a wider diet for your child and to help develop the skills of biting and chewing. It's also an important step on the road to shared family meals.

At first, usually between four and six months, the aim of weaning is to accustom your baby to different tastes and textures. Breast or formula milk is still providing an ample diet so don't worry if most of the solid food finds its way to anywhere but your baby's mouth. Baby cereals and vegetable and fruit purées are fine, although wheat-based cereals containing gluten could cause an allergic reaction at this stage.

Remember that your baby loves to be breast- or bottle-fed, safe in your arms. At first she may reject spoon feeding as different and 'unloving'. When you begin to wean, hold the baby in your arms and give a small breast- or bottle-feed first. Use a plastic spoon or even a clean fingertip and be content to introduce a minute amount into the baby's mouth. Let her savour the new taste. Smile and make encouraging noises and don't get agitated if your baby rejects this new and strange substance. Finish with another small breast- or bottle-feed and try again next time.

Some mothers prefer to use proprietary brands. Others make their own fresh purées each time, but it's safe to make larger quantities and freeze in small portions as long as it's done carefully. At this stage breast or bottle milk is still the most important part of the diet.

SIX TO NINE MONTHS

Between six and nine months of age, your baby will graduate to mashed or minced food, and wheat-based cereals can now be included. Bread is acceptable and finger foods such as pieces of fruit or carrot usually go down well because the baby sees this as independence. Homemade food is good because you can provide as much as your baby needs. Proprietary brands are limited on size and may not be enough as your infant grows.

Foods that might cause choking, such as peanuts, popcorn, chunks of meat and hard vegetables and fruit, should be avoided, but however 'mushy' the food, a tiny child should never eat without supervision.

NINE TO TWELVE MONTHS

Between nine and twelve months, babies learn to cope with most family foods although lumps need to be mashed. Your baby willstill need breast or formula milk between her three meals a day but bottles should be dispensed with by the first birthday because of possible dental problems.

Your baby may miss the bottle and if this is so, a dummy or soother can be a substitute, but avoid dipping it in sweet stuff. Ideally, a child shouldn't skip meals, especially breakfast. After a night's sleep energy levels are low and a breakfast of cereals with fruit and milk, an egg with toast and a drink of the child's choice will top up the necessary levels. Although some salt is essential to tissue fluids, it's best to use it sparingly. Babies should never have salt added to their food and toddlers should not be encouraged to want salty things such as crisps.

Once the process of weaning is complete, mealtimes should be enjoyable and not occasions for anxiety. Don't be alarmed if your child refuses one meal. Don't serve it up again; it doesn't become more palatable with time. Don't pile plates high with food. Huge amounts of food make a child feel pressured. Often, with a small child, presenting finger food is the answer. Mealtimes should be happy occasions, the opportunity to talk and relax, as much for children as adults.

A WORD ABOUT VEGETARIANS

Vegetarians must make sure they feed their babies a wide variety of food in sufficient quantity to supply their needs. Specialist advice on this is advisable.

If you're a vegetarian, you may want your baby to be one, too. Follow the advice on weaning and make sure the diet you're offering is adequate by talking to your health visitor or GP. It's best, too, to check out family history on both parents' sides to see if there's a history of asthma, eczema or nut allergy. If there is, it doesn't necessarily mean your baby will follow suit, but it helps to be forewarned.

Other allergies to eggs, wheat or citrus fruits may occur but these are easily dealt with by withdrawing the offending foods. In this, as in other problem situations, your health visitor can be your best friend.

The Picky Eater

Every child will be faddy occasionally over certain foods. If this is ignored it will usually pass, but if parents become obsessed with the need to include, say, sprouts or fish in the diet, then some children will become almost proud of hating fish and glow when you tell family and friends of the struggle to get fish down them. So try to rise above the conflict. Substitute a food with the same nutritional value and move on.

If your child is always food-resistant, don't let mealtimes become a battleground. Keep meals simple. Slogging for hours to produce cordon bleu won't necessarily produce an appetite. Make food attractive and don't worry too much about table manners. Eating finger food is better than no eating.

When you think there'll be no more progress, lift the toddler from his high chair or let the older child leave the table. There's nothing to be gained by keeping a sullen or weepy child in place. It means they will associate future meals with conflict. And never, ever act the Victorian parent and serve the rejected meal up next time.

Discuss menus with your child, whether or not there's a problem. Ask which vegetable would look nice with which type of meat or fish and allow the odd eccentricity. Combinations that make you gag may appeal to your child and allowing choice makes him feel in control and well-disposed towards food, especially if he can be involved in some small way in its preparation.

Of course, you can't allow a regular diet of jam sarnies and baked beans but you'll be amazed at how conventional children will become given free rein. Anarchy may rule for one menu but they soon revert to more normal combinations.

Never, ever force-feed. You'll end up hating yourself and your child will hate food. You can't help being anxious but don't let it show. Chat through mealtimes and avoid threats or bribery but it's allowable to show pleasure at an almost clean plate. If you become really anxious, talk to your doctor or a dietary paediatrician.

TEETHING

CHAPTER 11

A Gnawing Problem

Most babies don't have their first tooth until around the age of six months, although it can be much later. There are twenty milk teeth already in the gums when your baby is born and the process of their erupting through her gums can be painful. She may salivate a lot and will want to chew anything in sight. Some babies have a teething rash or looser bowel motions, but beware of putting everything down to 'teething'. It could be some other condition that needs a doctor's attention.

It may help to gently massage the gum area with a clean finger, and chemists can supply teething gels, but the most effective help is something hard and cold for your baby to chew on.

Teaching tooth care

Although milk teeth are only temporary (they loosen and fall out from the age of five), it's important to keep them free from decay as they act as a foundation for healthy second teeth. Avoid giving sugary drinks and foods and institute good cleaning as a fun game.

Use special children's toothpaste, let him copy your technique and always get your child to brush his teeth after eating sweets. From the age of three or four, regular dental checks make your child comfortable with the dentist and ensure that all is going well.

A VISIT TO THE DENTIST

Your child won't dread a visit to the dentist unless he picks up on your own anxiety, so ensure that you feel comfortable about your dentist and your own dental health. If possible, arrange an outing as a treat for later. Something as simple as a visit to the swings projects a child's thoughts forward beyond the visit.

Most dentists and their staff enjoy working with children. If your dental practice doesn't, change it. Don't be afraid to ask for advice about matters relating to teeth. Nutrition, mouth hygiene and the use of a dummy are all allied to dental health, and professionals welcome your interest.

Don't expect a problem. Most check-ups are just that: a chance to make sure all is well. Regular trips to the dentist will keep problems at bay. Those that do arise can be easily dealt with.

POTTY
TRAINING

CHAPTER 12

LEARNING CONTROL

Around the age of fifteen months, a healthy child senses when his bowels and bladder are emptying but he doesn't have sufficient muscle control to do anything about it. At eighteen months you can begin to sit him on the potty after meals. Make this an enjoyable thing rather than a chore and when he occasionally obliges give lots of praise.

Be prepared for him wanting to use the potty a lot, often without success, and discuss his successes with him. Never refer to failures. Gradually they will be fewer and by the age of two he'll go all day without a nappy. At two and a half his night-time nappy is often dry, and by the age of three and a half he may well be happy to have a potty by the bed or a light so that he can get to the toilet unaided.

Please don't start potty training too soon. An infant of less than eighteen months simply can't be trained and it's cruel to try. After eighteen months, make sure he knows where his potty is, give him time without a nappy on – and be patient.

Once a child is trained, occasional bedwetting may occur. Check that your child is not under stress of any kind. It's important not to be panicked by a set-back after training, nor should you be downcast if your child isn't perfectly dry as soon as your neighbour's. Every child is different, in this as in everything else. Their child may be more successful here, your child will excel at something else. Your health visitor or GP are there for just such an eventuality as this. Sometimes there can be a physical reason for a return to wet beds – for example, a minor infection which will respond to treatment.

Remember that your toddler is tuned in to your reactions. If he senses you are disappointed or made anxious by his failure, you risk creating the very tension which could have caused the problem in the first place. Don't pretend it doesn't matter. Aim instead for a cheerful acceptance that it did happen but can be dealt with. Show that you and he are in this together and will sort it out. This is a time to emphasize how well he does in everything else. Self-confidence will reinforce his determination to succeed.

And be careful never to discuss his bedwetting with anyone while he is present. That is not to suggest it is a 'guilty secret', but it is his business and not for general discussion. Even toddlers have their pride. Don't make a great thing of changing his bed, either – the less fuss the better. As a temporary measure you can return to lifting him and placing him on his potty just before you go to bed. Do this gently and lovingly so there is no suggestion that you have to do this because he has failed you.

HEALTH

CHAPTER 13

KEEPING YOUR BABY WELL

When you first look at your new baby a wave of panic can engulf you. How can something so small survive? And how can you cope with the enormity of caring for this fragile creature? Remember that babies were born and survived in the time of the cavemen, of the Great Plague and a host of wars. They are tougher than you think, and now there is an army of professionals available to help when needed.

Trust your health visitor. Listen to the advice of grandparents, professionals, and friends who have children, but above all, never underestimate your own instinct as a parent. If you think something is wrong and someone who should know says all is well, weigh their opinion against your gut instinct. If you're still unhappy, ask for a second opinion. A leading paediatrician told me that he believes mothers do have an instinctive awareness of their child's condition, so don't be afraid to use it.

AVOIDING COT DEATH

Fortunately, all the statistics are on your side. The overwhelming majority of children survive and flourish. Cot death, which frightens so many new parents, occurs rarely. Make sure your baby's room is warm but not too hot. Place her on her back to sleep and don't smother

her in blankets, although blankets are better than a duvet. Her feet should be touching the bottom of the cot so that she can't wriggle under the blankets, and don't use a pillow until she is two years old. Be cautious about putting soft toys in the cot.

There may be times when you take your baby into your bed but it's best to return her to her own cot to sleep. Avoid exposing her to cigarette smoke at all times. Be extra vigilant if your baby seems at all unwell and call a doctor if you feel uneasy. The risk of cot death exists between the ages of one month and five to six months.

MAJOR ILLNESSES

Conditions such as hypothyroidism or phenylketonuria will be detected by the thorough examination each child undergoes in their first week of life. If any adverse condition is detected, the appropriate treatment will be instituted at once, so if you work hand in hand with your obstetrician and health visitor you need have no worries.

Should You Immunize?

As your child grows and starts to mix with other children and adults, he will come in contact with various infections. Some of these can be guarded against by immunization.

Controversy over the triple vaccine known as MMR causes anxiety for many parents. Some experts believe the injection against measles, mumps and rubella (also called German measles) is connected with autism. The vast majority of experts dispute this, however, and the government recommends the triple vaccine for all children.

Not to immunize at all is foolish because diseases like measles and polio can be life-threatening. If you have doubts, discuss them with your doctor. Having the injections separately is an option, but this can be expensive; the MMR triple jab is all that is on offer from the NHS. If you do opt to pay for single vaccines, it's vital to make sure you have all three administered. It's easy to have one or two and forget the vital third.

The British Department of Health recommends that all children should be immunized against the following diseases.

- At two months: HIB, an influenza virus that causes a range of illnesses, including meningitis

- At two, three, and four months: diphtheria, whooping cough, tetanus and polio

- At twelve to fifteen months: measles, mumps and rubella

- At three to five years: diphtheria, tetanus and polio (booster)

- At ten to fourteen years: rubella (girls only)

- At ten to fourteen years: TB

- At sixteen: tetanus and diphtheria

- At fifteen to nineteen years: polio

WHEN YOUR CHILD IS ILL

If, in spite of all your precautions, your child falls ill, don't panic. Small children can be wan and prostrate one minute, running and shouting the next. Examine your child carefully for a rash. The menningitis rash will not disappear when a glass tumbler is rolled over the affected area. Other rashes will disappear and reappear when the pressure is lifted. Sometimes illness will produce a wheezing cough or a rise in temperature. Keep Feverscan in your first-aid box. These are heat-sensitive strips which can be held against a child's forehead to read his temperature. Aching limbs, headaches, dizziness and confusion are other possible symptoms.

If you need to call out a doctor, it helps to have details of the symptoms and the exact temperature. You'll get a quicker response if the doctor sees that you've taken sensible readings and are still alarmed. Saying 'He seems hot, doctor' isn't half as good as 'His temperature is 100 degrees'. Rises in temperature don't necessarily indicate serious illness. Sponging the child's face and body with tepid water will lower the temperature. Never use cold water and keep the child swaddled in towels or an absorbent cotton garment. It's vital to stop your child dehydrating so give plenty of fluids. If these are refused because of a sore throat, keep on persuading, offering whatever drink appeals.

Never give aspirin, which is dangerous for children, and go easy with paracetamol syrup. It's best to get a doctor's or health visitor's advice before dosing your children. At the height of a temperature or minor illness your child may be off his food. Homemade soup, ice-cream, egg custard or any sloppy food will be more popular than something which requires chewing.

Sometimes childhood illness causes vomiting – not the gentle possetting of babies after a feed but real sickness with retching and distress. If a child is persistently sick he needs a doctor as soon as possible. If it's simply one bout of vomiting, be reassuring. Being sick is not pleasant for anyone. Once the episode is over, a quiet, darkened room with Mum or Dad nearby will calm him down. Emphasize that he'll soon feel better and, if possible, divert him with talk of tomorrow or some treat ahead. It's important, too, to make sure he gets plenty of fluids to prevent dehydration, but stick to small sips at first so as not to trigger off another bout of retching.

If your child has to be admitted to hospital, don't take it as a sign that he is seriously ill; he may simply need facilities which are unavailable at home. It's worthwhile enquiring about first-aid courses. It's unlikely you'll need to use your skills on your child, but you'll feel much more secure if you know you possess them.

Treating scrapes and abrasions

The small cuts and grazes that come from boisterous play need washing and then leaving open. Avoid antiseptic creams and solid plasters. If there must be a plaster dressing, pick a porous one that allows the skin underneath to breathe. If there's bleeding press firmly down on the wound with a clean pad. If the bleeding doesn't stop, get medical help. Nosebleeds respond to pinching the nose firmly with finger and thumb applied just below the bridge.

Bee stings, nettles and burns

A few children are allergic to bee stings so watch them carefully for a few hours. With stings, make sure any soothing cream you apply is suitable for children, as some which include antihistamines are not.

When the inevitable moment comes that your child falls into a nettle patch, reach for calamine lotion and avoid saying 'serves you right'. Children are programmed to explore.

Everywhere a small child goes should be screened for fire or heat danger, but if burns or scalds occur reduce the heat immediately by plunging the area into cold water. Don't apply ointments, which make the skin soggy and prone to infection. Don't prick blisters, however huge. They're there to prevent infection.

CHOKING AND DROWNING

First-aid courses are also invaluable for teaching the techniques needed to deal with choking. Babies should be held upside down by the legs and patted on the back. Older children should be bent over and slapped between the shoulder blades. The technique of dislodging an object by standing behind and using clenched fists to deliver a sharp blow just below the victim's ribcage needs expert tuition, as does mouth-to-mouth resuscitation. If you arm yourself with a knowledge of first-aid techniques, you will feel more serene than if you feel ill-equipped to deal with emergencies.

If your child has swallowed a foreign object, take him immediately to an A&E unit. Difficulty in breathing, a suspicion that he has swallowed something noxious, or a fit or convulsion also need hospital treatment. A severe fall or blow to the head needs a period of medical supervision.

Remember that a small child can drown in just an inch of water, so keep an eye on a child whenever water is near. This includes simple things like buckets or ornamental fish tanks. Again, I must stress the importance of knowing how to deal with accidents with water, and if you can't teach him to swim yourself, take him to swimming lessons as soon as he's old enough to join your local class.

OTHER CONCERNS

As your child develops you may notice things which cause anxiety. Perhaps she is bright enough in conversation and yet has difficulty in reading and writing. Or maybe his skill with a ball may be less than that of his peers. Don't immediately assume the worst. Lack of progress in reading can be an early sign of dyslexia or it may be a hearing or sight impairment. It may simply mean that a teacher has failed to motivate your child.

If you feel your child is not developing as fast as others, talk to your health visitor or, if your child is at school or nursery, his teacher or carer. Tell them of your fears and ask for their opinions. Avoid letting the child know of your anxieties or discussing her condition with everyone who comes to the house. Children should never feel they are 'a problem'. If they have to go for treatment be honest with them and be calm yourself. A small child gauges danger by how scared you are.

If your child is diagnosed as having a disability or disease, contact one of the helpful organizations listed later (*see* 'Useful Information', page 173) so that you may be well-informed about the condition and whatever can be done to alleviate it. Don't be afraid to ask questions of doctors and therapists; they will understand your anxiety. Be careful, however, that the disability does not become the hub of family life. Do what you can to keep the family ticking over normally and encourage your child to excel in other areas than those affected. If children have a problem to overcome, the more self-confident they are, the better.

DYSLEXIA AND DYSPRAXIA

A child who has difficulty controlling a ball or whose work is untidy may have dyspraxia, a condition which used to be known as 'clumsy child syndrome'. It is due to interference with the signals coming from the brain to the limb concerned. It doesn't mean the child's intelligence is low, and both dyslexia and dyspraxia can be helped by therapy (*see* 'Useful Information', pages 182–7).

LEFT-HANDEDNESS

Around one boy in ten and one girl in twelve is left-handed. A baby will generally show no preference for either hand. It's only towards the end of the second year that she will start to favour one hand, although she may switch allegiance after a while. Generally, you can't be sure your child is left-handed until the age of three or four.

Being left-handed can be something of a nuisance at times, but it is certainly not a disability. Trying to make a child right-handed can be damaging and lead to problems with speech and reading. Left-handed scissors should be freely available at both nursery and school and, although extra effort is needed when learning to write, a left-handed child will soon catch up and be level with her right-handed peers.

NERVOUS HABITS

At some stage your child may develop a nervous habit such as twitching her nose, twiddling her hair, or grinding her teeth. It's best to ignore this at first. It will probably pass quite quickly. If not, talk to your health visitor or doctor but avoid drawing attention to it. If a child finds that an action produces an audience it's only natural that she should repeat the process.

NIGHTMARES

Nightmares, which usually begin at around four (but can appear earlier), can be caused by unsuitable foods such as cheese, or those with a high level of colouring and additives, eaten late at night. Disturbing television programmes can lead to uneasy sleep, as can a worrying incident through the day. Tell your child it was only a dream and stay with him until his is calm.

Night terrors, an extreme form of nightmares, are rare but frightening for both child and parent. In both cases there is no need to worry unless they become regular occurrences, in which case seek expert help.

PETS

The latest research shows that living with a family pet can be beneficial to a child, but if the pet was already installed, be careful not to make it jealous. Don't appear for the first time with a child in your arms. Make a fuss of your pet and then introduce the baby.

A pet will want to sniff the newcomer, so hold its collar and let it sniff away, but avoid letting a pet lick your child or anything the child will handle or put to its mouth.

If you have a cat, use a cat net on your pram or cot because cats like to sleep near a warm bundle and could obstruct your baby's breathing – as well as such proximity being unhygienic. Talk to your veterinarian about keeping your pet healthy in order to protect the health of your child. However amiable your pet appears, never leave it alone with a small child.

CRAWLING
& WALKING
CHAPTER 14

ON THE MOVE

You may long for your tiny baby to move. The first time that tiny head raises itself from the pillow, the first time he pulls himself erect, the first wobbly step: these are moments parents treasure. But from the first triumphant moment when your baby realizes he can manage to turn over, he can never again be left unattended on a high surface. On a blanket on the floor, far away from sharp corners or objects which might be pulled over, your child can gradually become mobile.

This happens at around nine months to a year. You can offer encouragement by placing a favourite toy just out of reach or by holding out your arms from a distance. Some children crawl, others 'bottom shuffle' or 'walk' from one advantage point to another. The moment when they at last stand alone is thrilling for a child. He will crow with delight before toppling over because he knows a milestone has been reached.

As soon as a child becomes mobile, parents can say goodbye to an easy life. Toddlers can move with the speed of light and hate to be frustrated. Try to create 'safety zones' – places where there are no breakable objects, floors are cushioned by carpets and nothing can be pulled over; then you can sit and relax while your child explores. Resist the temptation to fasten a child in a high chair or playpen too often. It may make you feel safe but it makes your child feel imprisoned.

When your child falls over – and this will happen quite often – be on hand to comfort but don't remark on the mishap. 'Oh, dear, you're always falling over,' however lovingly said, can make a child feel clumsy and eventually expect to stumble. Saying, 'You're so good at walking,' has the opposite effect.

Prepare for your child to fall in love with stairs. They have a fascination for toddlers. At eighteen months your child will probably go up on hands and knees or haul themselves up the bannister. Coming down is a bottom shuffle. At two he will take one step at a time, bringing the second foot up before attempting another step. At four he can mount stairs like a grown-up but will probably come down one step at a time. From then on progress is rapid. A five-year-old can hop, skip, run up and down stairs and climb anything in sight.

A parent's role is to encourage, keeping one eye on safety and the other on the child's self-esteem. I know the heart-stopping feeling that your precious baby is about to break his neck but a child who is not allowed to use his body to the full is a frustrated and eventually unhappy one.

There are other advantages to be derived from physical activity. When children are active they breathe more deeply, absorbing more oxygen. Digestion is helped and waste products more efficiently eliminated. Children who get plenty of exercise sleep better and coordination of eye, brain and muscles is improved. And don't worry that a child will get over-tired. Unless he is spurred on, the average child will alternate activity with periods of rest, throwing himself down to day-dream or listen to a story. Ten minutes later he'll be leaping around again, refreshed. It's important, too, that he gets into the exercise habit for later life.

Above all, remember that your child is unique and has a unique schedule of development. Because the child next door can catch or kick a ball at three and your child can't doesn't mean your child is backward. In all probability, your child is advanced in something else or is simply developing at a more leisurely pace. If you have real worries that persist, ask your doctor to check out your child or refer you to a paediatrician. He or she will quiet your fears or take steps to treat any condition which is holding back progress.

PLAYING

CHAPTER 15

The Importance of Play

At the very beginning a mother or father will play with a child because he can't manage alone. But the tendency is to draw back once the child can handle toys and bricks. *He's happily occupied,* you think. *I can get on with something else.*

That's a pity because research has shown that a parent's involvement can be beneficial. Your child learns by watching your techniques with Lego or dolly's buttons or poster paint and his confidence increases, but it's important not to do things for your child because you do them quicker. In addition, don't over-organize his play.

Jigsaws give great pleasure, but they are one-dimensional because they can only be played with in a way that leads to one conclusion. Building bricks can be roads or bridges, towers or train sets, and through them the child learns to use his imagination.

The role of television

Settling your small child in front of a television screen for long periods is frowned upon. Television should never be used as a baby-minder, but that is not to say that a brief exposure to it will bring the sky down. There is little or no stimulation in watching pictures flash across a screen, yet no one who has watched a one-year-old absorbed in the Teletubbies can deny their appeal.

My own view is that, used in moderation, television is a useful tool. If it keeps your baby happy while you prepare a meal or get ready for bath time that's fine, but it should never be seen as a substitute for the interactive play between baby and parent which encourages the development of all five senses.

Television can be a pleasant diversion for an older child, but if it becomes a child's only diversion it is counter-productive. It can easily become a battleground as children compete to view their choice of programme. This provides an opportunity to practise fair play if you help them to schedule their viewing so that each of them gets some of his or her own way. Try to offer an alternative diversion to each child when it's his turn to surrender the remote control and, if there's only one TV set, make sure Mum and Dad have their turns, too.

Sometimes there may be programmes you'd prefer your child not to watch. Try not to prohibit viewing as that can arouse a desire that might not have existed before the ban. Instead, plan some pleasurable family activity away from the screen.

TOYS

Some parents are disapproving of 'girl' or 'boy' toys. It's true that it's damaging to stereotype the sexes, but neither should we force children to play with 'the other sex's' toys. Provide both varieties of toys and let him or her choose.

Some experts believe boys are born with a predilection for aggression and girls with a leaning towards domesticity. My own view is that any such tendency is the result of generations of conditioning. Women were reared to be domesticated and 'nice'; men to be forceful and warlike. In a changed world we can allow our children to be themselves, so if your son wants to play dolls' tea parties and your daughter to disembowel a toy tractor, why not let them?

The same is true of aggressive toys. Telling your child that toy guns are forbidden will make them unbelievably desirable. However, some studies have shown that aggressive toys do encourage more hostile behaviour among children. I suggest that rather than ban them, you instead divert attention from them after a little while by proposing a more enjoyable and cooperative form of play. If this is vigorous and fun – for instance, a lively game of tag – the guns will soon be forgotten.

FRIENDS

Friends are an important part of play. Once your child is old enough to have playmates, he will learn cooperation. Although you must make sure that no child comes to physical harm it's best to let your child learn from experience. If he shares, others will share with him. If he is dictatorial, his friends will turn away from him.

It's sometimes painful for a parent to stand back and watch their child negotiate the minefield of human relationships, but the earlier that learning process begins, the happier your child will be. This freedom should also apply to friendships. It's important to give your child access to other children whenever you can as this will lead to friendships. If you don't like their choice of friend, ask yourself why. Unless real happiness is involved your child's choice should prevail. That's how he learns to judge character.

If you have twins, there may be a temptation to think all will be well on the friendship front. There is no doubt that there is a special bond between children who have shared a womb, but they should be encouraged to explore their differing potentials and have separate circles of friends. As mentioned earlier, often one twin will appear more vociferous and outgoing than another and will direct events for both of them. The dominant twin is not at fault, but parents should be wary that the less outgoing twin does not become introverted and almost a shadow of her stronger sibling.

Too often, parents assume that twins will be enough company for each other and make less effort to encourage friendships outside the home. Later, in their school lives, twins may need to go separate ways; if they are used to socializing independently from an early age, this will be easier.

IMAGINARY FRIENDS

Don't be alarmed if your child develops an imaginary friend at some stage. Imaginative display emerges in the second year of life. A toddler will use any object to represent a car or a train, a cuddly toy becomes a mother or a child, he drinks from an imaginary cup or smacks his lips at imaginary food.

At age three, imagination has extended to role-playing. He or she is a doctor, or a milkman, and if there are some dressing up clothes, an old handbag, and cheap jewellery, they can role-play to their heart's content. Watching your child pretending to be you can be a salutary experience. And allowing this kind of role-play frees your child to release aggressive impulses that might get him into trouble in a real situation.

Sometimes that imaginary friend can be a channel for your child to show you his emotions or to let you know that something is troubling him. For example, if your child tells you his imaginary friend is unhappy, that may be a way of introducing something he's embarrassed to talk about in relation to himself. If the imaginary friend has been naughty, that may mean he has been naughty and wants you to know it. There's no need for you to enter too far into the illusion, just don't dismiss it as 'silly'. It will pass in time.

BEING GOOD

CHAPTER 16

CREATING GOOD BEHAVIOUR

A parent who wants to keep his or her sanity needs a sense of humour. The difficulty is knowing when to see the funny side of something and when it needs to be taken seriously. When a disaster occurs — the breaking of a precious ornament, for example — a child has been punished enough by the shock of the incident.

TALE-TELLING

Another form of whinging is tale-telling. In a small child, tale-telling may have a purpose other than just being mean. Your child may be testing your standards. 'Jane's just taken a sweet,' may mean, 'Is it all right if I take one, or will you be cross?' Persistent tale-telling can be a sign of deep insecurity or fear of what may happen. All too often, the child's need is ignored as he is told not to be a tale-teller.

ATTENTION-SEEKING

Young children may go through a phase of attention-seeking and this can be wearing. They seem to have an inbuilt gauge that tells them exactly when to push your buttons and drive you to the end of your tether. When this happens, try to understand what is happening. Did you give her extra attention the first time she made a play for notice? If so, you are getting a learned response.

Most children crave the attention of the people they love best: their parents. If you only give your children attention when they are naughty, then you can be certain that they'll *be* naughty. Start to give attention spontaneously and for no reason other than that they are playing nicely or in a quiet mood. Once this is in place, ignore the attention-seeking by walking away to do something else; don't sit there coldly like a brick wall. Simply go off to wash up or cook or tidy a room.

Unless it's dangerous, don't reprove any form of attention-seeking, because reproof or punishment is, in a strange way, giving the attention the child wanted. If you lose your cool and scream, that can also seem like attention. So don't react with anger, however tempted you may be. This isn't easy, but if you stick to it, it will pay dividends.

SWEARING

Two things that distress parents are the use of bad language and answering back. Remember that, although children know this is naughty, they don't have an adult concept of what they're doing. 'Being cheeky' quite probably elicited a laugh the first time it happened because you were taken by surprise. Similarly, a word that causes you to jump immediately goes into your child's armoury. Show horror at the word 'chair' and a small child will regard it as swear word of the week!

Swearing, in a small child, has to be learned behaviour, and sometimes parents catch an uncanny echo of their own speech patterns. If your five-year-old says, 'I'm bloody fed up with this,' he didn't learn it from a nursery rhyme. With a small child, it's probably best to ignore the odd oath — although you should find out where they are being picked up.

CHEEKINESS

'Being cheeky' can be satisfying for a child who feels frustrated and hard done by. It's most likely to occur when a child thinks he's not being listened to or allowed to have a point of view. It's sure to recur if he sees it makes you smile! Don't respond to insolence but try not to make a big deal out of it. Say 'We'll talk when you calm down,' and move away. But be sure to keep your promise to talk and to listen. If your child learns which type of language and tone brings results, he'll adjust.

A child who obeys your every command without argument is simply giving you blind obedience and is not thinking things through for herself, so try not to feel threatened by argument or failure to obey immediately. You have the benefit of experience; you know what is right. Your child has to learn, and if questioning is seen as insolence, or at best, awkwardness, she will never learn. Of course, when your child responds to a request with 'Why?' it's a temptation to say 'Because I say so.' But that's an unproductive response. Explain why and you should get more cooperation.

When your child asks for something or permission to do something, try not to give a flat 'No'. Instead, say, 'I'm sorry, we can't do that now, but perhaps we can tomorrow.' If it's an impossibility, suggest an alternative. If it's a request for something dangerous or beyond your means, explain why it can't be done. If you treat your child with respect, he'll react more responsibly.

Although you have always to respect your child's individuality and rights, there will be times when, faced with a defiant child, your will has to prevail. It's best to avoid head-on confrontations. Instead, say, 'I'm sorry. That isn't going to happen,' and then walk away. If he threatens to go ahead anyway, deprive him of the opportunity to do whatever is in contention but don't harangue or threaten. It's important that you are sure of your own superior authority if you are to convince your child of it – so don't hammer it home.

When the episode is over, behave normally. Don't relish your triumph or feel the need to compensate them for losing. It's over now and best forgotten.

TANTRUMS

Tantrums can be a feature of early childhood. Sometimes a toddler will hold his
breath until a parent panics. This usually begins at around
eighteen months. A two-year-old knows what he wants and
needs to do, but something (sometimes you, sometimes his own
lack of capability) is stopping him. Anger erupts into fury, and
the child stops breathing. His face turns blue as the air supply
diminishes. It's a terrifying sight, but the moment the child
faints for lack of oxygen, his tongue muscles relax and he will
breathe again.

Remember that your child is as terrified as you are of these
uncontrollable emotions. Reaching out to give a gentle cuddle
can stop things coming to a head. Children outgrow breath-
holding, and if you handle them carefully, the tantrums will
cease. See them for what they are: attempts to make your child's
world the way he wants it to be. That may be annoying for you,
but it's logical on his part to try to make things work out his way.

Avoid tantrums by never saying 'No' unreasonably. For your
child to feel safe, 'No' must mean 'No' and never 'Maybe.' To say
'No' and then give in to a temper tantrum is re-enforcing the
idea that being naughty pays dividends. I know you love your
child to bits, and seeing him distressed is painful. But if you
really love him, you'll help him to realize that bad behaviour

doesn't pay. If you give in to a tantrum, you teach him that 'No' means 'Yes, but you must have a tantrum first.'

Avoid situations that may lead to tantrums. Your voice can be helpful here. 'Firm but loving' is what you should aim for. If you speak pleasantly but with enough conviction, you signal that tantrums will be a waste of time. Use diversion, too. Suggest a game or a walk, anything to take your toddler's mind off trouble. This is especially helpful later in the day, because tiredness is a frequent cause of tantrums.

Don't forget cuddles. A tired child contemplating defiance will often melt in a warm embrace and decide not to bother after all. Once in a tantrum, your child needs you to be calm. Sit down beside him to make sure he doesn't hurt himself, but don't intervene unless you have to for safety reasons.

When it subsides, say something quite unrelated. 'Shall we go and look for Daddy? or 'Will you help me sort these buttons?' will be more productive than 'We don't want any more of that, do we?'

BEDTIME

Bedtimes can be battlegrounds, especially when your child is tired but determined to win another half hour just to prove he or she can. It's natural for a child to want to stay where there's conversation and interest, but sleep is important, so you need to establish some rules. I believe in routine but not in inflexibility.

Turning off the TV five minutes before the end of a well-loved programme won't make for a restful night. Saying there isn't time for a story because it's one minute to deadline seems mean. You must guard against the gradual erosion of bedtime but don't feel your authority is at risk if you allow an extra five minutes now and then.

Small children like being tucked in and kissed goodnight, but if they're not tired it's better to let them sit in their cot with a well-loved toy or picture book. Go back in half an hour when they're asleep and you can remove the toy and tuck them in for the night. Older children may enjoy half an hour to read or listen to music.

However you play it, make bedtimes happy times. And never allow a child who has been put to bed to come back into the bosom of the family. Allow it once and it will be that child's constant aim in future. If they need reassurance after a dream or a scare, go to them rather than have them come to you.

POLITENESS

We all want our children to be polite, partly because we want to be proud of them, but mainly because politeness will ease their passage through life. The best way to instil politeness in children is to set an example. If you are polite to them, they will respond; as they respond to you, so will they behave with others. Encourage them to be respectful of the old and protective of the young. Whether or not you're an animal-lover, show a reverence for all life. From such things is politeness born.

It's nice to see children behaving graciously, but beware of expecting too much too soon. A small child, offered a plate of cake, will study the size of portions and opt for the largest slice. This is normal behaviour. At that age, it's logical to put your own interests first. In time, as he comes to enjoy sharing, he will become generous. If your behaviour towards him is generous he will see this as an adult and superior way to be.

STEALING

Some forms of behaviour are more important than simple manners. Stealing and overtly sexual behaviour trouble parents greatly. A child of three or less does not fully understand ownership. He may get upset when a friend purloins one of his toys, but will happily bring home someone else's toy car. This action has no malicious intent, and it is important to realize this. 'Jamie will miss his car,' is all you need to say, because that is a concept your child can grasp. He will return it because it makes sense to soothe Jamie's distress.

At five or so, a child understands that stealing is wrong, but he has a strong sense of his own needs. If a friend has a bag of sweets and he has none, it seems natural to redress the balance. You have to explain possession and point out that what is his is his, and he wouldn't like to lose it. So it is for everyone.

LYING

Lying tends to get some parents into a lather, as many are convinced that it is a sign of moral turpitude. Very young children don't lie consciously; they have difficulty in distinguishing fantasy from reality. Most small children will lie if they sense they are in trouble, even when they've been caught red-handed. It is usually only after the age of three or four that a child develops moral awareness and knows what a lie is. If you severely punish lying, the likelihood is that your child will simply try to lie more effectively next time.

The imaginative lie – 'There's a witch in the wardrobe' – isn't a lie at all and should be treated as the play-acting it is. And explain white lies to your child if you use them yourself. She'll understand the need not to hurt someone's feelings. Above all, explain why lies are counter-productive. Never, ever threaten to withdraw your love.

SEXUAL CURIOSITY

Sexual curiosity is natural in a small child. Remember that, to a child of two or three, a penis is no more or less interesting than a nose or an ear.

Boys of pre-school age can have erections and derive some satisfaction from what they see as a phenomenon, but this is not a sexual act to a child. His body is simply changing before his eyes. This is interesting, but it is certainly not erotic.

Fifty per cent of children under five engage in genital handling, and some children masturbate. Parents find this embarrassing because they see it as sexual behaviour, but in fact, the child derives comfort from it, not sexual stimulation. It equates with thumb-sucking in that it is soothing. Your child will only begin to attach sexual connections if it sees that you are alarmed and disturbed by this particular action.

Don't exhibit anger or punish him if you see him masturbating. Ask him gently not to do it and then change the subject by providing a diversion. If you don't succeed and your child becomes preoccupied with sexual handling, consult an expert, because this can be a sign of stress.

SMACKING

It is impossible to discuss behaviour without referring to smacking. Some experts would like to see smacking made illegal. I don't agree with that view because I think it would inevitably lead to the courts intervening in family life just because good mums or dads lost their temper once in public and found themselves in trouble. This would benefit no one, certainly not a child. But that doesn't mean I approve of smacking. A child who is habitually smacked or beaten is the victim of abuse, for which there are existing legal constraints.

If you smack your child because she smacked her brother, you confuse her. He annoyed her, so she smacked him; she annoyed you, so you smacked her. Where's the difference? Smacking also diminishes a child's sense of guilt over a wrong action. She feels she has 'paid the price', so it's OK. If you smack, you may encourage your child to lie his way out of trouble. Also, never smack your child for what you see as a 'sexual' offence, such as masturbation or sexual curiosity. That only links sex with punishment in the child's mind, and this can be damaging in later life.

Although I don't think a well-loved child is doomed because his mum or dad once tap his bottom when he runs into the road or throws his sister's favourite toy into the loo, I do think smacking should be avoided. Instead, explain why such actions are wrong. He may get run over! How would he feel if his sister disposed of his toy? Find other ways of punishing him if you must, but never withdraw your love. And never give dire warnings of punishments you both know you'll never carry out. What you threaten, you must do, so think first.

Trying to understand your child's thought processes is the key to dealing with behaviour. Don't set impossible standards, whether it's over tidying his room or playing with friends.

Decide where you need to make a stand and where you should turn a blind eye. If you constantly chide your child, he will cease to listen. If your complaints are rare, you'll receive maximum attention. Don't issue ultimatums unless you mean them. When you do, you must carry out your threat. But beware of breaking that small spirit that is your offspring. Very few offences merit that.

Staying safe

For your children to feel secure, they must have confidence in their own ability to cope in some difficult situations. They can't have this confidence unless you have allowed it to develop. This means standing back, biting your tongue, while they learn by trial and error. Your wanting to protect them is entirely natural; you are programmed to feel that way. But just as you must not help the chick out of the egg, so you must draw back from too much cosseting of your child.

In order to have peace of mind for yourself, prepare in advance. Teach your child road safety and enquire whether or not your local police force runs any kind of safety schemes. Make sure that whenever he is away from you, he knows where you are, knows his own name, address and telephone number.

Of course, a very young child will never be away from you unless it is in the prearranged care of someone you trust, but children can and do get lost in crowded stores, at sporting events, funfairs or in other situations involving lots of people. Tell them that, if they do happen to get lost, they should stand still and wait for you to find them rather than stray further in search of you.

It is vital that children trust police officers, but small children may not be able to distinguish between one uniform and another, so this instruction must be approached with caution. Warn them not to go with anyone, however friendly they may seem, but instead, to ask the grown-up to find you and bring you back to them. And above all, make sure that they stand still in a place where there are lots of people milling around.

It is important to stress that strangers in cars are to be avoided, but much child molestation is carried out by people known to the child, so don't overplay the 'wicked stranger' theme. Give them a back-up source of help, such as Grandma's phone number, and tell them that no friendly adult who says they've come on mum's behalf will mind if they check first. Some parents use a family password, but if this should get into the wrong hands, it can give a child a false sense of security.

Explaining to children that there are people who might harm them is difficult, but in this day and age, it can't be shirked. Even so, try to avoid giving the impression that the world is full of monsters waiting to do terrible things to children.

I told my son that there were a few sad people who might want to steal him away to live with them. He wouldn't like this, we would positively hate it, and therefore we must make sure it never happened. This approach made him cautious but not apprehensive of every stranger he met. It also has the advantage of not depicting abductors as 'wicked-looking' people – something which can make a child vulnerable to a predator who happens to look 'nice'.

TRUTH ISSUES

One of the most difficult decisions you will face as a parent is when to tell your child the truth. I believe you should never lie, because once caught out, your child will never trust your word again.

However, it's usually not necessary to deluge children with every detail of the truth. When they ask about items in the news that distress them, be prepared to discuss, but point out that bad things occur rarely and are unlikely to happen to them. This is a good opportunity to state why there are rules about playing outside and coming home or staying close in crowds. Once you're sure they're satisfied, take their minds off the subject with a diversion, but never distract them at the beginning. They know they're being fobbed off, and that only increases their fears.

Children are acutely aware of tensions in the home, so, if you know they've heard a marital row, be honest. Saying, 'Yes, I'm cross with Daddy, but I still love him' is reassuring. Saying, 'Don't be silly. There's nothing wrong' is not.

Visits to the doctor or dentist are another area where being truthful is difficult. I had vowed never to lie to my son, but saying, 'Yes, the injection may hurt a little bit,' wasn't easy. The benefit was that when I said 'This won't hurt at all', I was believed. Praising your children is vital, but keep the praise within the realms of truth.

Telling them something they've done is perfect when it is not is as counter-productive as constantly running them down. Be constructive in both praise and criticism and they'll come to value your opinion.

CENSORSHIP

Television sometimes displays images that are difficult for a child to cope with. Try to anticipate when there are programmes you don't want your children to see. Don't announce, 'You're not seeing that,' but arrange some diversion to keep them away from the screen.

MOODS

Accept that your child may sometimes feel fed up. It helps to be honest about your own moods. Unless you're a superb actor, you won't be able to hide how you feel, so it is better to say 'I feel a little miserable today because...' and then enlist their help to cheer you up. If you are worried about something, then explain, but keep it in proportion. Stress the actions you can take if the worst happens. This not only calms their fears, but it encourages them to look for coping strategies themselves. Remember that almost nothing you can tell your children can be as bad as the image they conjure up in their imaginations. Be truthful and trust your instincts in knowing how far to go.

TALKING ABOUT SEX

I believe sex education should begin in infancy. Telling your baby how much you loved carrying him or her inside you before birth is laying the foundations. A small child will accept that a baby needs to be kept safe, and where better than a mother's tummy?

Let your child see a newborn and explain that it needed protection and grew from an egg until it was big enough to emerge. If the next question is 'How did it get out?' explain. The truth will do: that a mother's body has a special place which expands when it is needed and thus allows the baby to be born.

Use proper names like 'vagina' if you're happy with them. The trick is to remember that you're explaining a miracle, so let your enthusiasm show. To a child, there is nothing 'dirty' about sex or birth. We infect children with our prurience as they grow, so describe the functions of a mother's body in pregnancy as you would explain a sneeze or bending and stretching. They are all natural processes.

It is extremely unlikely that a question about conception will follow immediately. It will come eventually, but try not to anticipate it. When you do have to answer it, remember to explain that it, too, is a natural process, but one that should belong to adulthood.

Explain the importance of preparing a home, or a 'nest', for the baby before conception. Explain how you and your partner (or you alone, if you are single), looked forward and made sure that you had a safe place for a baby. Adoptive parents can explain their longing and how hard they searched to find the right child to love.

Emphasize that the making of a baby is a loving action between grown-ups. It can be a joyful experience to see a child absorb this knowledge – almost gleefully because that is how they came to be and that's a good feeling. If you're a single parent with an absent father, explain that conception came out of love, but then you went your separate ways.

In sexual matters, as in everything else, don't give an untrue answer you will have to retract, such as 'You were found under a gooseberry bush.' It will cause complications for you, and it isn't fair on your child.

RELATIONSHIPS

Joyful family gatherings linger in the memory and can be a rich part of our life experience. But family life can also be a minefield. For every parent who craves the help and involvement of grandparents, there are others who see such involvement as interference or a refusal to let them assume their proper parental status.

GRANDPARENTS

Each family must make up its own rules about the role of grandparents, but if possible, such a role should exist. For some grandparents, the new birth can seem like a chance to be parents again. They experience the same level of wonder and joy they felt at the birth of their own children, but this time they have knowledge and experience they didn't possess then. It's not surprising, therefore, that they may be tempted to interfere. To a new parent, such interference may at first be comforting – but be careful. A child should only have one set of parents, and too much intervention, however well-meant, can undermine the fragile confidence of the new parent.

Whatever the difficulties within a family, the advantages of a good grandparent-child relationship far outweigh the disadvantages. Even after divorce, it's best to keep up links with both sets of grandparents. They are part of the mosaic that is your child's life. It is a pity to have missing pieces, unless family friction rules out the possibility.

One of the most important responsibilities of parents and grandparents alike is to ensure that the child they love can go happily out into life. Spoiling a child is self-indulgent, and ultimately harmful. Children who know that Gran will countermand Mum's rule, or that their own parents will bend to their will, expect that kind of treatment at school and later in life. When the world isn't so forthcoming, these children feel rejected, and considerable emotional damage can ensue.

This applies not only to treats or breaking rules; it also applies to conversation. Children love attention, especially from a parent. A toddler who wants to impart some fresh information will take his mother's face in his hands and physically turn it away from whoever she is talking to in order to possess her full attention.

No one wants to discourage a child's communication, but saying, 'In a minute, darling,' and finishing your conversation will let him see that he must take his turn for attention. It's vital, however, that as soon as possible, you do turn to him. That teaches him that waiting politely pays off.

SIBLING RIVALRY

The feeling that your brother or sister is really the advantaged one occurs to every child at some stage. 'She always gets more than me' or 'You let him get away with anything' are common cries. Rows over who goes at what time are the accompaniment to many bedtimes. The eldest child frequently feels put-upon; the youngest child resents being the baby of the family; middle children struggle to establish a place.

This can be painful for parents, but accept it as part of family life. Listen to all those cries of 'It's not fair!' in case there's a grain of truth in them. Answer reasonably. 'He doesn't have to wash up because he's too young to handle crockery' will produce a better response than 'Because I say so.'

Making comparisons can fuel sibling rivalry. However much you might like child number two to be like child number one, don't let those words pass your lips. Nor should you expect your child to follow a family tradition. Going to university to pursue the career of your choice is one thing; doing it only because 'Everyone in our family goes to university' is sad.

Be scrupulously fair about sharing out treats.

Although it's important to be even-handed with your children, you must also be aware of differing needs. One child may need lots of cuddling, another may not. Try to give to each what is needed. This is not showing favouritism; it's accepting your children as individuals. And because they're individuals, they need their own time with you. This can be difficult, especially if you're a working mum, but it is never impossible. Take one child when you do the supermarket run. By listening on the journey there, you'll learn more than in hours of group conversation. Make separate bath times with younger children, or have one of them help you in the kitchen. And praise each child's achievements whenever you can.

Above all, recognize that your children are lucky to be part of a family. It's natural that there will be jealousy sometimes or feelings of resentment, but learning how to control these feelings within the family is wonderful preparation for life in the outside world.

CONFIDENCE

Initially in the home and then at school, children must find their own place. Some children have a natural impulse towards self-assertion. Others are almost afraid to take a leading role. Some of this second group will become bossy in an effort to establish some sort of control over the situation they fear. It's best to leave children to sort out these situations, but be watchful.

The naturally assertive child may need help to understand the desires and needs of others; the self-effacing child may need his confidence boosted; and the 'bossy' child needs to feel safe in his world. All these interventions should be subtle, and if possible, made away from the scene.

Talking to your child during bath time or while walking in the park and discussing what goes on in group play is more helpful than wading in at play and telling Johnny to pipe down and Jennifer to stick up for herself.

In stressful situations, making eye contact with your child can be helpful. It signals, 'It's OK. I'm here but you can cope.'

In all situations, remember that your child is an individual. What he or she needs from a situation may not be what you would want in that situation. Your child must grow and develop his or her own potential. He can never be a second chance to realize an unfulfilled ambition for you or for grandparents. If this achievement of potential is to come about, your child must learn to make choices from an early age. Of course, you must apply common sense if safety is involved, or if the choice made could have irrevocable consequences, but in most other matters, children can be allowed to decide for themselves.

Like every mother, I've hovered, terrified my children would be hurt or humiliated, but I've tried to let them do their own thing whenever possible – even when I knew it might have disadvantages.

A NEW BABY

A new arrival can unsettle a first-born who's been used to having her mum and dad to herself. A young child may think,  'Does that mean they've tired of me?' It's as well to delay telling her a baby is on the way, because to a child, nine months is forever. But tell her before she's likely to hear it in conversation or in whispered asides, or before your tummy is big enough to push her off your knee.

Once the baby is born, make sure visitors speak to her before they speak to the baby. Have a present for her to give the baby and one for the baby to return. Make changes in her routine that emphasize her importance. A few minutes later at bedtime, time to spend with her mum and dad while the baby sleeps... such little things can ease doubts that she's being supplanted. And let her help with the baby chores of nappy-changing and bath time.

A child's position in the family can influence personality. A second-born can feel constantly behind a first-born, especially if that first-born is clever or gifted. A middle child can feel 'nowhere' compared to being the eldest or the spoiled 'baby' of the family. Wise parents avoid such pitfalls by seeing their children as individuals and making sure each is the centre of attention some of the time.

Most children go through a period of shyness at some stage. Build up confidence by emphasizing what they have to offer and what they're good at and encourage them to be helpful to other children who may feel the same. But don't go on about their shyness until they believe it's a cross they're destined to carry forever, and never mention it to other people when they are present.

Teach your child 'opening strategies': what to say to strangers or how to offer a toy to share. Don't take the easy way out and avoid group play. Yes, your child may have difficulty at first, but retreating only intensifies the problem.

Never underestimate your own role in your child's self-confidence. Each time you listen to what she has to say with interest, you are saying 'Your opinions matter. You are important.' I know how difficult it can be to concentrate when you have one eye on the cooker and the other on your watch, but laying the foundation of your child's future matters more in the long run than most day-to-day affairs.

Don't fall into the nagging habit. 'You're always dirtying your shoes' or 'Why do you make so much noise?' are off-the-cuff remarks with little venomous intent, but they can give unconfident children the impression that they're a drag on you. It is better to reward than punish, but the reward may be simply 'I knew you'd be able to manage that,' which implies your trust in their ability.

Another confidence-booster is to allow the child a degree of control over her own affairs. 'What do you want to wear today?' or, 'Do you want to keep your toys here?' is enough. And if you can let her extend that choice to family affairs, all the better.

'I was thinking of putting that clock over there. What do you think?' is emphasizing the child's place in the family hierarchy as someone with the right to an opinion. Sometimes that opinion will prevail and the advice be followed. Sometimes it won't. And that 'win some, lose some' formula is another valuable lesson.

CRISES

A small child has no experience of survival, so a crisis can seem like the end of the world. Helping children through crisis and teaching them coping strategies is vital, and yet too often their emotional needs are neglected in favour of attending to their physical wants.

Children packed off to neighbours in the wake of a family death may be safe, warm and fed, but their overwhelming impression is of a world – their world – in disintegration. They are seldom 'better off out of it' unless there is the chance of real physical danger – and unless the place they are going to is familiar and as much like a second home as possible.

Try to keep their routine and their surroundings as normal as possible. And be sure to explain what is happening and why you may be sad or on edge. Again, just as with protecting them against the dangers of abduction or abuse, there is no need to go into great detail, but do be prepared to answer their questions.

DEATH

It is tempting to indoctrinate your children with your own religious beliefs, especially when someone dies. Saying, 'Grandma has gone to Heaven,' comforts you both if you have a religious faith. In this area, you should obey your instincts. If you choose, you can say 'I believe' or 'I don't know,' but in either case emphasize that what has happened is part of life.

Remind your children of happy times and how much they were loved by the one they have lost. 'Grandpa always liked you to be happy' is a statement that is both true and comforting, and it allows a child not to feel guilty about having fun in the aftermath of death.

Above all, try to keep life as normal as possible. Of course, this does not mean that you should pretend that there has been no loss; it simply means that children need a sense of continuity. If you cry, don't apologize for it, but let them see that tears eventually dry and that nice things still happen. If you can, find a way to celebrate the person who has left the family scene.

In the wake of his father's death, I took my young son to a place we had loved to visit as a family. It was both painful and cathartic and allowed us to talk freely of the pain of the present, our hopes for the future, and how important a part Daddy would still play in our lives.

DIVORCE

When lives are disrupted by separation or divorce, make sure the child is prepared. All too often, children aren't told until Mum's or Dad's bags are packed and waiting in the hall. Allow children time to adjust, but never suggest that the parting might never happen. Emphasize how much cooperation there will be and the advantages of having two residences. As man and woman, you may be separating. As parents, you never can.

HOSPITAL

When illness strikes or children have to be admitted to hospital, it's important to stress that their place in the family will remain. Talk about plans for their bedroom when they return; show them a visiting roster and tell them exactly what family members will be doing while they are away.

With small children, a 'mystery' parcel to be opened at the end of visiting can be a useful antidote to tears on parting. Make sure the nursing staff know your child's likes and dislikes and the name by which he likes to be called. Be patient with moods or tantrums. Being in hospital can be a scary experience even for adults.

LOSS OF A PET

When a well-loved pet dies, stress how happy its life was and how it will never be forgotten by the family.

When a pet goes missing, the situation is more difficult. Show that you have done your best to find it and then point out that there is a good chance that someone, somewhere, will take it in and love it, too. While this may or may not be true, it does help a child to know that organizations exist that help lost and stray animals.

LOSS OF A TOY

If a well-loved toy is lost, search diligently, but if it cannot be found, say that someone probably has found it, and will love it as we loved it. A child needs a resolution.

DISABILITY

Self-confidence is particularly important for children who have a disability or a chronic illness. If they know that their inability to perform certain functions is matched by a talent in other directions, it will do much to compensate. Knowing their opinion matters gives them an equal status within the home. Make full use of the organizations that exist to help parents in this situation. You'll find them listed on pages 182–7.

USEFUL INFORMATION

REGISTERING A BIRTH

Every baby born in the United Kingdom must be registered by one of its parents with the registrar of births and deaths for the district in which the child is born. In England and Wales, registration must be made within forty days of birth; in Scotland, within twenty-one days.

Whoever delivered your baby will give you a birth-notification form to pass on to the registrar. If you're not married, your partner must also be there to put his name on the birth certificate. You need a name for the baby in order to register it, but you can change it later, should you wish, for a small fee.

Once the name of your child has been registered, you can start claiming child benefit. Get a claim form from your local Social Security Office.

If, for some reason, you should lose your child's birth certificate, you can get a replacement (for a small fee) either by going to the public search rooms of the General Register Office:

Family Records Centre
1 Middleton Street
London EC1R 1UW

or by applying by post to:

General Register Office
Smedley Hydro, Trafalgar Road
Merseyside PR8 2HH

You can also find out information about certificates by phone on 0870 243 77 88, or via email from certificate.services@ons.gov.uk.

PARENTAL RESPONSIBILITY & RIGHTS OF ACCESS

In the UK, a natural father has no legal right to parental responsibility if he is not married to the mother and his name isn't on the birth certificate (this may change when the Adoption and Children Bill goes through Parliament).

A father can acquire parental responsibility if the mother agrees, or by obtaining a court order. If the absent father maintains the child, that does not mean he has parental responsibility unless he fulfils the criteria just described.

Once a father has acquired parental responsibility, he would automatically become the child's guardian in the event of the mother's death. Seeking legal advice about a parental responsibility order can save future arguments.

In matters of access, the Lord Chancellor's Department has produced a parenting plan that can help; Family Mediation can also play a useful role. If there has been physical or emotional abuse, get legal advice before a difficult situation develops. If you don't already know and trust a solicitor, talk to the local Citizens Advice Bureau. Remember that a father who does not have parental responsibility (*see* above) has no automatic right to access.

If you are completely alone and have to relinquish custody of your child while you go into hospital or recover from illness, Social Services can help. Your child must be returned to you when you ask (unless there is a court order forbidding this), and you retain parental responsibility during the separation. Before contacting Social Services, it is helpful to contact the Family Rights Group or your local Citizens Advice Bureau. In all matters involving single parents, the National Council for One-Parent Families can help (*see* page 185).

I have been a single parent and I know the strain of being 'on duty' for twenty-four hours a day, but the moment comes when your child becomes a happy adult. Then you know the effort was more than worthwhile.

CHILD CARE

Some mothers will want or need to go back to work when their baby is still quite young. There's a tendency to look on child-minding as a modern phenomenon but, in fact, childminding began with the onset of the machine age and today it is estimated that something like a quarter of a million children in this country are cared for by child-minders.

Some parents prefer to employ a nanny to work in their own home but this can be expensive. Some couples opt for the father becoming a full-time carer. This is a matter for individual couples but it pays to consider the father's future when he is no longer needed in the home and his role as carer must not be secondary to the mother's role as bread-winner. If both parents are happy with the arrangement this can be a rewarding situation. A father gets to know his child and mother has the peace of mind that comes from knowing her child is in the most loving of hands.

Before you leave your child with a child-minder or nanny, however highly recommended, you need to know quite a lot about her. Will your child be her sole charge or is she caring for other children? Is there enough space in her house and garden for all the children to play freely? What experience or training has she had? What equipment and play material does she provide? Does she set aside time to cuddle or read to each child? Above all, is her house clean and safe? What other adults will have access to the children because they live in her house? Does she offer a nourishing and attractive menu?

Under current legislation someone who looks after a pre-school child in her own home for pay is required to be registered with the local authority, and this means that they must conform to certain standards. However, that does not absolve the parent from vigilance or necessarily mean the childminder is without flaw.

Only some of these questions apply to nannies, and the parent will provide the safe and happy environment, but nannies' references need to be thoroughly checked. In time she may become almost a family member, but parents should still conduct spot-checks and listen carefully to what their child's words or behaviour tell them. Good nannies and childminders will appreciate a parent who is interested enough to ask questions and carry out spot-checks.

In no circumstances leave your child with anyone he does not know well. Take time to make your child feel comfortable with the person who is going to take your place, even if this is a grandparent or aunt. There can be nothing more scary for a child than to feel he has been abandoned to strangers or someone he saw fleetingly the week before. Discuss your requirements and standards with your nanny or childminder. For instance, how do you want them to deal with naughtiness if it occurs? What about potty training or feeding habits? He's your child so your will should prevail, but childminders, even doting grandmas, are not machines. They have standards and opinions, too, and the best way to sort this out is by co-operation.

Children learn by imitation so it is inevitable that your child will pick up some of the habits and emotions of a person with whom he spends his day. That is why it's important that you leave your child with someone of whom you fully approve. And a certificate or qualification doesn't mean that person is right for your child.

Some mothers need to employ childminders for school-age children. Try to find someone who is prepared to do more than just walk your child home from school and stick them in front of the TV. Although you will talk to your child later in the day, he may need to unburden himself when school is over, and needs a listening ear.

NURSERY

When the time comes to find a nursery place, some of the same rules apply. Sadly, there may not be a wide range of nursery provision in your area but shop around if you can. It's better to have a longer journey to nursery and a happy child than bring a weepy or sullen child home from just around the corner. You need to trust the staff, especially the person in charge, and you need to be frank about anything in the home which may upset your child. Your child also needs to know that the two adults who control his or her life are cooperating, especially over matters such as feeding and lavatory training.

A good nursery will not simply 'mind' the children. It will stimulate them and prepare them to enjoy being part of a group. Staff should also talk to the children in their care, encouraging conversation and ensuring that children can talk freely about anything that troubles them.

WORKING MUMS

Leaving your child for the first time can be painful. Try not to feel guilty. Helping your child to make relationships with others is vital. As long as you have done your best to provide good care see it as an important part of your child's development. However, if leaving a young baby makes you unbelievably unhappy, do everything you can to go back to work later or work part-time. Often, women have to juggle a desire to stay with the baby and maintain their standard of living. This must be an individual decision, but weigh things carefully before you decide.

Helpful Organizations & Support Groups

Association for Post-natal Illness
+44 (0) 207 386 0868

BLISS (Premature babies)
+44 (0) 870 7700 337

Breast Feeding Line (NCT)
+44 (0) 870 444 8708

British Allergy Foundation
+44 (0) 208 303 8583

Careline
+44 (0) 208 514 1177
For parents and children.

Child Benefit Centre
+44 (0) 8701 555 540

Child Support Agency
+44 (0) 8457 133 133

Childline
+44 (0) 800 11 11

Children's Legal Centre
+44 (0) 1206 87 38 20

Contact a Family
+44 (0) 808 808 3555

The Child Psychotherapy Trust
+44 (0) 207 284 1355

The Cot Death Society
+44 (0) 845 601 0234

Council for Disabled Children
+44 (0) 207 843 6061

CRY-SIS
+44 (0) 207 404 5011

Dyspraxia Foundation
+44 (0) 1462 454 986

Families Need Fathers
+44 (0) 207 613 5060

Family Contact Line
+44 (0) 161 941 4011
For parents with children from baby to school age. Provides flexible services to relieve family stresses, especially if feeling lonely or isolated.

Family Rights Group
+44 (0) 800 731 1696

Fathers Direct
+44 (0) 207 920 9491

Gingerbread Advice Line
+44 (0) 800 018 4318

Homestart
+44 (0) 800 068 6368
Help for families under stress.

Kidscape
+44 (0) 8451 205 204
Bullying helpline.

Look (The National Federation of Families with Visually Impaired Children)
+44 (0) 121 428 5038

Maternity Alliance
+44 (0) 207 588 8583

The National Autistic Society
+44 (0) 870 600 8585

National Childbirth Trust (NCT)
+44 (0) 870 444 8707

National Child-minding Association
+44 (0) 208 464 6164

National Council for One-Parent families
+44 (0) 800 018 5026

National Family Mediation
+44 (0) 207 485 8809

National Society for the Prevention of Cruelty
to Children (NSPCC)
+44 (0) 808 800 5000

NHS Direct
+44 (0) 845 46 47

ParenTalk
+44 (0) 700 2000 500

Parentline
+44 (0) 808 800 2222

Pre-school Learning Alliance
+44 (0) 207 833 0991

SANDS (Stillbirth and Neonatal Deaths)
+44 (0) 207 436 5881

Single Parent Action
+44 (0) 117 951 4231

Twinline
+44 (0) 1732 868 000
Helpline for parents of twins, triplets or more.

Twins & Multiple Birth Association
+44 (0) 870 770 3305

Young Minds
+44 (0) 800 018 2138
For children with emotional or behavioural problems.

INDEX